# THE
# LOW CARB
# FAST FOOD
# *Diet*

Carla Gray

NutritionNetwork

SA PL

# *The* **Low Carb Fast Food Diet**

Every effort has been made to ensure that the information in this book is complete and accurate. However, variations in nutrient value, menu changes, and errors and omissions can occur. The ideas, theories and suggestions in this book are not intended as a substitute for consulting with your physician.

Printed in the United States by Fidlar Doubleday

Book design and editing by Rebecca Hayes at Cedar Hill Publishing

Cover design by Nicole Valdes

Second printing with updates, July 2004.

ISBN 0-9755534-0-2

Library of Congress Control Number: 2004108676

*For more of our products, go to:*

**www.LowCarbFastFoodDiet.com**

# Table of Contents

# Before You Begin

One of the most important pieces of advice any weight loss book can impart is to **see your doctor for a complete physical evaluation.**

Beginning any diet or exercise program has potential risks and there is not one perfect medical solution for 100% of the population. You may have specific needs that will require your doctor to put you on a weight loss plan low in saturated fat rather than a low carb diet, which is traditionally high in saturated fats.

Contradictory medical studies exist that arrive at a diversity of conclusions. Some studies show that a low carb diet that is high in fat can increase cholesterol levels and potential health risks. Other studies have shown good news for carb counters. A May, 2004, study showed a low carb diet lowered triglyceride levels (blood fats linked to coronary heart disease.)*  New studies will continue to emerge. It becomes apparent why the role of your doctor is vital in sorting out which information is most important for your individual medical needs.

The purpose of this book is **not** to convince you to eat exclusively at fast food restaurants or to begin a low carb diet plan. The goal of this book is to give you information you can use if you choose to eat at fast food restaurants. Also, if you desire to begin a low carb diet, the information in this book may be helpful in understanding the fundamentals of limiting carbohydrates in your diet and in making wise food choices. Please remember these important facts: moderation in all things, and consider your doctor as your diet-partner. If you *are* going to eat fast food (like most of us), make it your weight loss friend, not foe. Good luck and good health!

---

* Researchers at the Veterans Affairs Medical Center in Philadelphia found in the largest study of its kind that dieters on low carbohydrate plans had greater improvement in their levels of triglycerides than traditional dieters. The same study showed that at six months the low carb group had lost an average of 13 pounds, the conventional dieters lost about 4 pounds.

# Part One

# *Introduction*

You know you have done it in the past. You know you will do it again, maybe even tonight. You might not talk about it, but you *will* keep doing it.

What is it, this incredible, little secret? Fast food! You and millions of other Americans will eat in a fast food restaurant today. You are going to do it, so do it right.

Consumers are bombarded by news stories blaming fast food restaurants and lazy lifestyles for America's rising obesity epidemic. You hear it on the radio and see it on the evening news. America is struggling with fat. You hear the message. You understand the problem. You begin the next day afresh, intending to "eat healthy" or stick to a diet plan.

But, your day might look something like this…

You skip the breakfast bagel and feel proud of

yourself. But, before you even arrive at the office, you are stressed by the morning traffic, the disagreement with your spouse and the rowdy kids you dropped off at school. Still, you skip the usual donut during coffee break and feel smug about how your new diet is proceeding.

But watch out. Before noon, the job, the co-workers, the phone calls and the boss start getting to you. Suddenly, you hear that voice whispering in your head and you rationalize.

"No time for lunch; I have to meet that 3 pm deadline for my boss. But I'm starving. I'll grab a double cheeseburger just for today. Tomorrow I can get back on my plan. If I hit the drive-thru before 11:15, I can beat the lunch crowd at Wendy's. I know - forget the burger, I'll order a salad, because it is better for me. Now, which of their dressings has the least carbs? Low Fat Ranch sounds good. Maybe Honey Mustard is better... I don't *think* mustard has calories, but what about carbs? I am so confused!"

And the guilt sets in.

Evening approaches, and so does the voice. "I am so tired. I was swamped all day at work. I should cook. That soup I made on Saturday is full of vegetables, but it doesn't sound very exciting right now. If we have it for dinner, the kids will complain. Still, it has to be better for us than take-out." You grab a bag of chips to eat while you decide...

And so, Day One of the diet has been sabotaged by the little voice. What's worse, you feel guilt along with that sense of another diet failure.

Well, don't despair. The book you are holding in your hands will give you the key to a weight loss strategy that is revolutionary. It combines the hottest weight loss trend in the country, low carb eating, with the realities of our hectic lifestyles. The resulting *Low Carb Fast Food Diet* not only works to melt off the pounds, but as an added bonus gives you more time for friends, family and relaxing, the things that truly matter in your life.

**How *The Low Carb Fast Food Diet* Is Organized**
This book is divided into two parts.

**Part One:** This section gives an overview of the prevailing theories and techniques of carb counting. To help you along, you will also find a full week's worth of easy-to-follow low carb fast food meals. All you have to do is order and eat.

When you have seen the sample meals, take a look at "The Good, the Bad and the 'Holy Cow'." The name says it all. Even veteran carb counters will be surprised at the dieter's fast food choices. Nearly every restaurant has appetizing options that won't blow your weight loss progress, even though the foods sound like they would be diet poison. Likewise, carbs come in so many different forms that they can hide out in unexpected places. You'll find plenty of surprising carbohydrate counts in the most innocent (sounding) foods.

As a bonus feature, low calorie information is provided in Chapter 5 for the times when you are with calorie-counting friends or family.

**Part Two:** Estimating a food's carb count can sabotage a diet. For example, experienced carb counters know that the sliced onions that go on a burger have almost no carbs. Therefore, it is not too much of a stretch to assume that frying those same onions in carb-free oil and eating a large order of Sonic onion rings would not be *that* bad for the daily carb count. But one look at the **Carb Chart™** in this section tells a different story. Compared to an order of regular Burger King french fries (a notorious high carb food at 46 carbohydrate grams) those onion rings tally a steep 102 grams of carbohydrates. Who knew? Not many, without the **Carb Chart™**.

In this section you will find the read-at-a-glance **Carb Chart™**, a tool you will refer to often. It contains nutrient values on over a dozen of your favorite fast food restaurants. In addition to carbohydrate counts, you will find values for calories, fat, fiber, sodium and cholesterol as they exist at the time of this book's publication.

For restaurant menu changes and updates, make regular visits to www.LowCarbFastFoodDiet.com.

Now, whether you drive-thru alone or eat with family, friends or co-workers, you can plan ahead when going out to grab a meal. Plus, with the **Carb Chart™**, you will eliminate one of the most common reasons given for diet failure: impulse ordering based on nutritional guesswork.

*The Low Carb Fast Food Diet* will be the easiest weight loss program you have ever tried. No cooking. No shopping for strange foods that end up moldy in a corner of your refrigerator. The work has been done for you. Simply drive to the take-out window or order home delivery. Sit back, relax and *lose weight*.

# Chapter One:
# Eat Fast Food and Lose Weight…
# Really!

Do you want to:

- Lose weight?
- End food cravings?
- *Burn* body fat instead of *storing* it?
- Have more free time than ever before?

If your answer is a resounding "yes" to any of these questions, then *The Low Carb Fast Food Diet* is for you.

You can eat until you are full and still lose weight. Measuring foods, controlling portions, and trying in vain to ignore gnawing hunger pangs can be your diet history.

But wait. The voice in your head says that the chicken you throw on the grill and the salad you put together out of your own refrigerator is somehow healthier than the one you get at the drive-thru. Dispel that myth.

Today, fast food restaurants recognize that over 70% of their customers want nutritious, diet-compatible meals. Fast food restaurants have changed for *you*. Now you can use them to change yourself, your health and your waistline.

**Why go Low Carb?**
Low carbohydrate diets and eating plans are everywhere in our culture today. Why is there so much emphasis on this phenomenon? In a recent Harvard weight loss study, low carb dieters were allowed to eat an additional 300 calories more per day than those on other weight loss plans. Instead of losing less weight than the other dieters, the low carb group lost the same number of pounds while eating significantly more food - an extra 2100 calories a week. No wonder dieters are jumping on this bandwagon.

Is there some sort of metabolic magic that happens when cheese, steak and olive oil replace baked potatoes and bagels? That appears to be the case. In fact, there is more than one theory in the medical community behind the success of a high protein, low carbohydrate diet. For example, a study at Arizona State University discovered that body temperatures actually climbed after a high protein meal compared to a meal high in carbohydrates, a function known as thermogenesis. Heat is good. It indicates increased metabolic function. That translates into an increased number of calories burned.

Protein → Increased Temperature → Calories Burned

Today, many scientists believe that, when your body needs energy, it will first look for carbohydrates as fuel. That means your body is searching for sugars and starches, like bread and potatoes. Do you have those in your current diet? Give them the boot.

If those carb sources aren't there, your body breaks down your fat reserves. Your body actually prefers burning fat. So, help your body do what it wants to do. Your fat-burning system will choose that extra fat supply over all other food types… except carbs. It's up to you to eliminate excess carbs. The proteins and vegetables you eat will be digested and used for their nutrients. You *should* lose weight… *if* you do not provide your body with all those carbs.

**Fast Food vs. Home Cooking**
For many people, less time in the kitchen can have a significant impact on weight loss success. Just looking at a favorite carb or calorie-dense food can cause your brain to release dopamine. Dopamine is a chemical associated with reward and craving,

according to researchers at Brookhaven National Laboratory. The condition is explained by our biology. Through the ages, the urge to eat was reinforced in humans. Eating was the means of storing fat as a defense against starvation during times when food was not plentiful. In the process of preparing your diet-conforming meal, even a glance at a "forbidden" food can trigger the cycle of hunger and cravings again, adding needless hurdles to your weight loss program.

With *The Low Carb Fast Food Diet,* you are not only out of the kitchen more, but eating low-carb meals, as well. Hunger and portion control will be part of your past. Now you can eat until you feel full and satisfied. You will enjoy delicious, filling meals each day, with *no cooking*, *no grocery shopping* and *no dirty dishes,* and you can be dropping pounds by this very time next week.

Can you cook at home? Of course you can. The beauty of this program is that fast food eating can be combined with home cooking. You now have a choice. Are you in a hurry on the way to work? Drive-thru, but keep a copy of this book in your car. Simply select a low carb breakfast and order. You packed yourself a lunch last night? Great! Zap it in the microwave today at the office and enjoy. Oops... forgot to thaw out something for dinner? No problem. Simply drive-thru, but open *The Low Carb Fast Food Diet* first to be sure you are making good low carb choices before you order.

## Life in the Fast Lane

Until recently, low carb fast food seemed about as likely as vitamin-enriched candy canes. Fortunately for us, it's easier than ever to have it your way, as powerful forces converge to create major changes in the drive-thru lane. The trend is being fueled by the popularity of low carb diets. Restaurants are responding. How? By making menu revisions. Now, most fast food venues accommodate America's changing eating patterns. Your favorite fast food restaurants can provide tasty, varied meals with freshness, convenience and low carb selections.

Just as you know where you are headed when you set out for the drive-thru, you need to know your diet destination when you begin your weight loss journey. When you eat fast food, you will be carb smart with the **Carb Chart™** (located in Part 2 of this book). You can avoid diet blunders that may actually cause you to gain pounds. Surprisingly, salads are not always the best option, but you wouldn't know that without the **Carb Chart™**. For example, look at the following lunch options.

| **Lunch Option A** | **Lunch Option B** |
|---|---|
| Taco Salad with Salsa<br>Small Coke | Chicken BLT Salad<br>Creamy Ranch Dressing<br>Extra Chicken Filet<br>Large Diet Drink |

Most dieters would choose Option A and believe they have made a wise decision. But in reality, Option A has 113 carbohydrate grams, while Option B has only 15 carbs. Surprised? Having the **Carb Chart™** with you means you can follow a dieting strategy that keeps you abreast of the choices you need to make. Keep this diet detective within arm's reach.

Look back at the actual numbers for those salads. Would you have guessed you could so innocently sabotage your diet? It doesn't have to happen again.

The chart is full of eye-openers. Hidden carbs, calories and fat are revealed in other innocent, healthy sounding foods that can unravel even the best diet plans. Use the up-to-date guides in this book to create your own fast food plan that can protect you from unknown slip-ups. To help you along, you'll find easy-to-follow meal examples, in which all the work has been done for you. All you need to do is order and eat. Enjoy the extra free time to do something for yourself.

But, you may have an obstacle to overcome first…

**Lifestyle Evaluation: What is Your Guilt Level?**
Have you ever felt uneasy while picking up dinner at the drive-thru? Perhaps you experienced a nagging of your conscience. Is it your

responsibility to prepare a nutritious meal every day, and you simply can't do it? No time or no desire, the result is the same - guilt.

Are you susceptible to Fast Food Guilt? Take a moment to check:

o I feel guilty when I serve myself and/or family fast foods.

o I sometimes hide the fact that I've eaten a fast food meal.

o I want to feel good about what I eat and what I serve my family.

o Growing up, we had a home-cooked meal almost every night.

Do you have guilt that you did not realize? Is ordering fast food difficult for you? Once you realize that you are in the driver's seat with the nutritional information in this book and the **Carb Chart™**, you will know what items to order. Should you still feel remorse because you choose from a menu instead of a refrigerator? No! Make a healthy plan for those times you drive-thru, then enjoy a nutritious meal without the side order of guilt.

**Now What?**
What's next, now that you know this information?

This is the optimum time for you to see your doctor and get a baseline assessment of your current weight and tests such as cholesterol and blood pressure. Later, you can use those facts to determine how much your health has improved. You will also be able to see significant progress in moving toward your weight loss goals.

Beginning any new diet is the ideal time to have a discussion with your physician. No book can possibly cover all of the individual medical conditions known only to you or your doctor. In fact, your health care provider may help you identify stressors and factors that may hinder your weight loss progress. Also, studies continue to emerge that can impact your doctor's advice for your specific needs.

The information in this book is based on medical and nutritional approaches backed by research at the date of this publication. Medical breakthroughs will continue to occur as new research validates or contradicts current treatments. So, visit your doctor and get ready for a thinner, healthier you.

# Chapter Two:
## The Skinny on Low Carbs

It's not uncommon for a non-dieting individual to consume up to 300 grams of carbohydrates per day! In the real world, this means that if you eat a garlic bagel from Dunkin' Donuts, you will have consumed 79 grams of carbohydrates. The bread is first converted into glucose which is released into your blood stream as sugar. When blood sugar levels become elevated, your body is flooded with insulin, an essential hormone. It is, however, the amount of insulin that counts. Excess carbohydrates, which can produce dramatic, unhealthy spikes in blood sugar, cause the body to supply *too much* insulin. The unwanted result of this process can be stored body fat and *increased hunger.*

Most people, especially those who fight weight gain, love carbs. Carbohydrates range from breads, pastas and grains to fruits and some vegetables. Sweets, snack foods and sodas are loaded with them. What factor do these diverse foods share?

The way the body reacts to them. Excess carbs cause insulin surges and result in weight gain for most people. However, there are millions who have an even stronger reaction to carbs.

## Your Body on Carbs

There is a reason why some of us are more sensitive to the lure of carbohydrates than others, and it has a name: carbohydrate sensitivity. Just as we are individuals with different eye and hair color, we each possess our own unique metabolic responses to foods. Medical research is substantiating what many of us have suspected a long time: being overweight is not solely a function of overeating. Former Surgeon General of the United States, C. Everett Koop, M.D., has observed that part of the U.S. population is "carbohydrate-sensitive."

What does this term mean, and how does it affect you? Could this be why you struggle to lose weight and fight food cravings? Do you *want* to change your eating habits but feel like you can't? Have you found that you crave specific foods, and now you understand… they are carbs? You are not the only one with these questions and facing these struggles. Others can also tell the story of how hot crusty bread, chocolate chip cookies or salty chips take on addictive qualities.

Take a look at the following Lifestyle Evaluation to

assess your physical responses to foods. Your answers could show more than a simple hunger-eating relationship between you and your next meal. Your answers could help identify whether or not you are carbohydrate-sensitive.

**Lifestyle Evaluation: Food Relationship** – check any statements that apply to you.

o When I eat a starchy food (like bread), I am hungry in a couple of hours.

o Sometimes when I begin to eat carbs (ice cream, snack foods, donuts and candy), I have a difficult time stopping.

o I get grumpy or tired in the afternoon and a snack makes me feel better.

o I nibble anytime there is food available.

o I sometimes lose control over my eating.

o If I feel irritable or grumpy, eating makes me calm.

o I occasionally experience "brain drain" and unexplained anxiety.

o At times, I crave a specific food (chocolate, bread, sodas, sweets).

If you checked more than three statements, you may be carbohydrate sensitive. From a metabolic standpoint, you are likely storing fat when you eat carbs. You might even feel controlled by carbs. Your body may be taking a front row seat on that sugar roller coaster, a ride that can cause irritability, fatigue and food cravings.

**Cravings**
Terrible feelings of guilt and remorse often accompany a carbohydrate-sensitive person's food compulsion. You probably thought your snacking routines were plain old habit. Who considers that sugar and white flour (junk food) might be another form of addiction? Yet, look at the results of indulging in carbohydrates:

- Quick energy boost
- Feeling of comfort
- Eventual feeling of guilt
- Eventual feeling of remorse
- Decision to stop indulging
- Fighting the cravings, again

Have you ever noticed the results of eating carbs are temporary? Once you begin to eat a high carb food, your body's production of pleasurable brain chemicals quickly begins, and your blood sugar starts to spike. Just as rapidly, the brain chemicals recede, and your blood sugar plummets from insulin response. The process is over, and once again, you hunger for even more junk food. The sugar roller coaster ride never seems to end if you feed yourself what you are craving – more high sugar carbs. That ride, just like your brain chemistry, gets out of sync. Your cravings kick in, and one donut is never enough.

How can this be? It is a simple principle of chemistry.

High carbohydrate intake results in a metabolic process (you are probably not aware of it). This chemical change could be the primary reason for the difficulty you have in altering your eating habits.

Think back to a time you really tried to change the way you eat. Perhaps that time is as close as your last New Year's resolution. When you consciously decided to change your eating habits, you probably developed some serious cravings within a few days. In addition to the cravings, did you experience irritability, confusion and fatigue as you tried to alter your eating patterns? Perhaps you were a statistic to a metabolic chemical equation.

Carbohydrate Intake → Sugar → Insulin Surge
= Irritability, Fatigue and Food Cravings

High carbohydrate foods are metabolized quickly. They enter the bloodstream and rapidly elevate blood sugar levels. The elevated blood sugar levels trigger a surge of insulin running through your body. The physiological result triggers new cravings. The good news is that, when you eat foods that take a long time to break down, such as protein and low- or non-carbohydrate foods, insulin is released gradually. Consequently, blood sugar and energy levels are constant, so your mood evens out, the fatigue vanishes, and the food cravings stop.

The solution to blood sugar swings is to stabilize your blood sugar. You can do this by cutting your carb intake. When you begin this process, you may find you have some form of withdrawal, like any addict. Do not let yourself give up. Hang in there for a few days. Once you get through the initial withdrawal phase, your hunger and cravings should pass. In fact, most people find that, once they shake off the carb-sugar habit, they feel no strong desire to go back. They have more energy and feel better than they ever imagined. If you expect this withdrawal reaction when you change your eating habits, stick to your plan through the few days. Your metabolic reactions will soon change, and you will come through this phase with a much more comfortable weight loss experience.

On *The Low Carb Fast Food Diet*, you will be losing weight while indulging in a variety of appetizing, fulfilling foods. Try eating an abundance of non-starchy vegetables, beef, fish, chicken, pork, cheese and salads with rich dressings, while slashing carbohydrates such as sweets, potatoes, pasta, starchy vegetables, bread (that means no croutons on those salads) and most fruits. *You will not be hungry.* You will be on a weight loss plan that is revolutionizing the way people think about diets.

In a study conducted at Washington University, volunteers ate a low carbohydrate diet with calories coming predominately from proteins such as chicken and fish. The protein was accompanied by salads and vegetables. Over the course of the study, individual low carb dieters were given an *extra 25,000 calories* compared to dieters on a low fat program. That should have added up to seven pounds of weight gain. But for reasons even the researchers did not fully understand, it did not.

**Proteins**
Simply put, proteins are more filling than carbs or fat. Proteins, therefore, cause us to eat less. Eating less means losing weight, as long as you are not eating excess carbs.

Each day, your body uses up protein derived from the food you eat. You need a continuous supply of protein-rich foods in order to function well. Protein delivers extreme nutritional and metabolic assets to your body. Protein helps your body make new cells, synthesize neurotransmitters and maintain body tissues.

Inadequate protein, on the other hand, leads to a

drop in your immune response and an increased risk of factors for illness and infections. Without enough of this vital nutrient, your body will eventually break down and digest the proteins in your own cells and tissues, which include those in your muscles. Muscle strength and mass then decline. Of course, you want the exact opposite, for muscle mass is the furnace that burns far more calories than fat.

Protein's effects on your body, such as leveling out blood sugar and insulin levels, help to close the sugar roller-coaster ride. Protein is the hero, insulin is the culprit. Many in the medical community now accept the theory that when found in extremely high levels, insulin can cause obesity. Furthermore, insulin can promote the development of diabetes. Heart disease, hypertension, polycentric ovarian syndrome and breast cancer have also been linked to this sugar versus insulin war. Thankfully, when excess carbs, insulin levels and sugar surges are reduced, health can improve. You should begin to store less and burn more of the fat in your body.

That's a lot of information, but there is a primary formula to remember:

Excessive Carbs → Elevated Blood Sugar
Elevated Insulin → Excessive Pounds

## High Carb Foods
Now that you know the effects of excessive carbs,

take a quick look at some examples of foods that are high in carbohydrates:

High starch vegetables (such as potatoes)
Grains
White flour
Chips
Bagels
Donuts
Sugar and sweets
Sweet Sauces (such as honey mustard, BBQ sauce)
Rice
Beans
Fruit
Condiments (such as ketchup and pickle relish)

Do you have servings of any of the foods on the above list in your current menu? It's time to remove them from your diet. Remember, on *The Low Carb Fast Food Diet* you are replacing those high carbs foods with surprisingly delicious and filling alternatives from your favorite fast food restaurants.

## Net Carbs

The latest evolution in low carbohydrate health is the concept of Net Carbs. This idea came from the Atkins program. There is a type of carbohydrate that exists, such as fiber, sugar alcohols, glycerin and organic acids, that are thought to pass through your body without causing blood sugar spikes. These are called Net Carbs. Net Carbs appear to have little effect on a jump in insulin production inside your body and do not cause the same metabolic responses that initiate weight gain.

**Induction Phase**
Some of the low carb diet plans on the market today include an induction phase. This is usually a time period of no longer than two to three weeks when carbs are pared down to a bare minimum, approximately 20 grams per day (about the amount found in one ear of corn). Carbohydrate foods are slowly increased after the induction period is over, until your weight loss reaches a plateau. Your own acceptable carb level will depend on factors such as age, body type, exercise and gender. There is an active debate in the medical community about exactly how many carbohydrates are the correct amount to consume for weight loss. Some physicians do not think that the same carbohydrate restrictions should apply to everyone and believe each dieter should have an individual medical evaluation.

Because of these conflicting theories, this book does not address the induction phase of the low carb diet. Rather, it serves to guide you towards sensible weight loss and into lifetime weight maintenance.

**A Suggestion**
One time-tested method of determining your daily carb level for weight loss is to keep a food diary for 5 or 6 days. This process establishes your pre-diet

baseline. No one has to see it but you, so write down everything. Include that sneak attack you made on the candy machine at the office or that beer you just happened to stop for on the way home from golf. If you succumbed to KFC fried chicken, french fries and an apple pie…record it. Then, sit down and take some time to add up your daily carbs. Average it out to how many carbs you ate per day during your recording phase.

Now get that calculator out and reduce that daily total by 25 percent. Take your total number of average carbs per day and multiply by 75% (x 0.75). The result is the number of carbs you should eat per day to begin weight loss. As always, be sure to check with your doctor to see if this would be a safe level of carbs for your individual nutritional needs.

It is a good idea, once you begin your weight loss program, to record what you eat on a daily basis. This will effectively track your carb intake, and it will help you make adjustments to your eating plan as needed. Once you know the number of carbs you should be eating to lose weight at a healthy pace, all that is left to do is a little advance planning.

By the way, don't forget to get some exercise (an evening walk around the neighborhood or a few laps around the office parking lot at lunchtime will do wonders for speeding up your weight loss). Drink plenty of water too.

## Staying On the Band Wagon

Once you develop your plan and begin new eating habits, how will you stick to it? There is hope. People find that, once they eliminate the carbs, they feel no strong desire to go back to them. A diet approach that allows them to eat a rich variety of meat, fish and salad, prepared with butter, cream and cheeses, is a heavenly indulgence. After a few days on a high-protein regimen, most people stop suffering from carbohydrate cravings and are released from the blood sugar roller coaster.

A typical meal of grilled fajita meat with shredded cheese and sour cream, topped off with a salad covered with guacamole and spicy dressing, feels like anything but deprivation. Not surprisingly, sheer hunger is the reason most often cited for giving in to cravings. It is nearly impossible to go hungry eating like this. And the variety is endless.

Those on a high protein diet typically lose twice as much weight as people on a high carb weight loss program. So toss the bread, ditch the rice and throw away the chips. Forget you know the word sugar, and take a look at the foods in the next section. Choose your favorite fast food dishes from the following pages. They will rev up your metabolism, turning you into a fat-burning machine.

# Low Carb Meal Choices
## LUNCH
*Carbs are measured in grams*

| Wendy's | Boston Market | KFC |
|---|---|---|
| Small Chili Shredded Cheese 2 Strips of Bacon | Marinated Grilled Chicken Green Beans Vegetable Medley | Original Breast without Breading Mashed Potatoes |
| 22 grams | 13 grams | 16 grams |
| **McDonald's** | **Wendy's** | **Subway** |
| Bacon Ranch Salad with Chicken Newman's Own Ranch Dressing | Chicken BLT Salad (no croutons) Creamy Ranch Dressing Extra Chicken Filet | *Atkins* Turkey & Bacon Melt Wrap with Monterey-Cheddar Cheese |
| 12 grams | 14 grams | 11 net grams |
| **Burger King** | **Taco Bell** | **Arby's** |
| Shrimp Caesar Salad with Creamy Garlic Dressing) | Chicken Soft Taco Supreme | Low Carb Southwest Chicken Wrap |
| 17 grams | 20 grams | 15 net grams |

# Low Carb Meal Choices

## DINNER
*Carbs are measured in grams*

| Arby's | Subway | Boston Market |
|---|---|---|
| Martha's Vineyard Salad with Ranch Dressing | *Atkins*- Turkey Breast & Ham Wrap | Chicken Noodle Soup ¼ Dark Chicken |
| 26 grams | 10 net grams | 10 grams |
| **Arby's** | **Chick-Fil-A** | **Subway** |
| Market Fresh Wrap Ultimate BLT | 4 Chicken Strips, Side Salad and Bleu Cheese Dressing | *Atkins* Chicken Bacon Ranch Wrap |
| 17 net grams | 19 net grams | 8 net grams |
| **Boston Market** | **McDonald's** | **Burger King** |
| Rotisserie Turkey Steamed Vegetable Medley Creamed Spinach | Chicken Nuggets (6 piece) Bacon Ranch Salad | Low-Carb Angus Steak Burger with Bacon and Cheese |
| 20 grams | 35 grams | 7 grams |

Now that you have seen the wide array of low carb meals, you will realize that you have choices not excuses. You will also notice that by increasing protein and decreasing carbohydrate intake, your appetite should decrease. The low carb option gives you a metabolic edge so significant that most people produce a steady weight loss, even if they have experienced dramatic failures or regained weight on other diets.

These facts mean *The Low Carb Fast Food Diet* might be just the right meal ticket for you.

# Chapter Three:
## The Good, the Bad and the "Holy Cow!"

Change is difficult. How many times have you tried to change your eating habits, but never achieved the results you hoped for? Now, it is easy to accomplish your diet-compatible goals if you know where, how and what to order.

You can get high quality lean protein, soups, salads and vegetables at fast food restaurants today. Choices including juicy grape tomatoes, carrots, cucumber slices, green pepper strips, fresh-cut apples, dried cranberries and baby spinach all await you at the corner drive-thru. When you have this many choices, you end up with more variety than in many home-cooked meals.

The main reason often cited for the popularity of the carb-based diet is the simplicity of the formula. Toss the bun and your body will ignore the quarter-pounder. For the most part, it really is that easy.

Carb-conscious dieters often think, "I already know what is good and bad for me to eat."

A recent study showed, however, that most people on low carbohydrate diets *do not* know the actual number of carbs they consume in a single day. In fact, test subjects ate considerably more carbohydrates than they estimated. Why? Because hidden carbs are everywhere.

Even innocent, low-starch choices can be tricky. Think about it. When was the last time your made-from-scratch meal came with a complete nutritional breakdown that included carb counts? Contrary to traditional wisdom, eating at home can challenge your carb-smart strategy more than eating at a fast food restaurant, *if* you know what to order. When you use the **Carb Chart™**, (in Part Two of this book), the menu math is done for you. No more guesswork.

**The Good and The Bad**
What about the hidden pitfalls in a low carb diet? It's time to test your carb savvy! Read through the following fast food items and guess the number of carbs. Write your answer in the blank provided. (The *real* answers are at the end of each grouping.)

**Boston Market**

1. Southwest Grilled Chicken Salad & Fire Roasted Tomato Bisque Soup _____

2. Hearty Chicken Noodle Soup & 1/4 dark Rotisserie Chicken _____

3. Marinated Grilled Chicken, Small Seasonal Fruit Salad & Green Beans _____

4. Grilled Mango Chicken, 15 Vegetable Soup & Butternut Squash _____

5. Hand Carved Rotisserie Turkey, Steamed Vegetable Medley & Creamed Spinach

_____

6. Meatloaf with Creole, Mashed Potatoes & Corn

_____

**Answers:** (1) 71 (2) 10 (3) 23 (4) 75 (5) 20 (6) 85

**Burger King**

7. Sausage, Egg & Cheese Croissant & small French Fries _____

8. Low-Carb Angus Steak Burger with Bacon and Cheese _____

9. Double Whopper w/ Cheese & Large Size Onion Rings _____

10. Scrambled Eggs, Bacon & Sausage

_____

11. Tender Crisp Chicken Sandwich & Large French Fries _____

**Answers:** (7) 53 (8) 7 (9) 113 (10) 1 (11) 115

**Subway**

12. *Atkins* Turkey & Bacon Melt w/ Monterey-Cheddar Cheese _____

13. Garden Fresh Salad w/ Croutons & Red Wine Vinaigrette _____

14. Steak & Cheese Classic Sub & Vegetable Beef Soup _____

15. Grilled Chicken & Baby Spinach, Greek Vinaigrette _____

16. 6" Meatball Sandwich _____

17. Chicken Bacon Ranch Wrap w/ Swiss cheese

_____

**Answers:** (12) 11 "net" (13) 36 (14) 64
(15) 8 "net" (16) 53 (17) 8 "net"

**Wendy's**

18. Spicy Chicken Sandwich, Side Salad & Fat Free French Dressing _____

19. Small Chili w/ Shredded Cheddar Cheese & 2 Strips of Bacon _____

20. Taco Supremo Salad & Small Frosty

_____

21. Three Chicken Strips, 1 pkt. Deli Honey Mustard Sauce & Caesar Side Salad

_____

22. Chicken BLT Salad w/ No Croutons, Ranch Dressing & Extra Grilled Chicken Filet

_____

23. Mandarin Chicken Salad, without Rice Noodles, without Oriental Sesame Dressing, One Packet Almonds & Creamy Ranch Dressing

_____

**Answers:** (18) 83  (19) 22  (20) 91  (21) 51  (22) 15  (23) 26

How did you do?  Did you say, "**Holy Cow!**" at some of the answers? Don't feel discouraged if you were off on many items. If your calculations were not quite right, you have learned valuable new information.

Make your life easier and carbohydrate counting more accurate. Use the **Carb Chart™** to quickly locate your meal choice and see how the carbs add up. If an item does not fit in with your daily carb allotment, you will know immediately. (Maybe you can save that treat for another day.) Next, simply scan the sections of menu items and find a choice that fits.

**Simple Guidelines**
To help you understand the way a low carb diet should be put together, here are a few general guidelines:

**When eating at Subway:**
- All sandwiches can be made with their delicious wraps. Wraps contain only 5 grams of Net Carbs.
- Choose a 6 inch bread, and you'll have a carb count ranging from 35 to 48 carbohydrates for the same meal.

**When eating at Burger King: (BK)**
- BK Burger without the bun contains approximately 5 grams of carbs, depending on the condiments you choose.
- If you skip the ketchup, you save 3 grams of carbs per burger.

- Regular Ranch Dressing has the same number of carbs as their Hidden Valley Fat Free Ranch Dressing.

**When eating at KFC:**
- Beware of a few side items. Cabbage, a low carb vegetable, is great for your diet. Coleslaw, on the other hand, contains 22 grams of carbs.
- Just as bad, one biscuit is 23 grams of carbs.
- Mashed potatoes with gravy total 18 grams.

**When eating at Pizza Hut:**
- Pizza Hut offers a wide range of toppings that include several vegetable and meat choices. These choices are a great addition to any low carb diet.
- Whether you dine in or out, double the toppings and do not eat the crust. Enjoying your pizza without the dough will keep you within your day's carb range.
- If you must have crust, choose their Thin N' Crispy. A large slice of Stuffed Crust Cheese Pizza will usually rack up 43 carbs per slice. Thin N' Crispy has just 20 carbs per slice.

**When eating at Long John Silver's:**
- Their chicken sandwich contains 40 carbs. Instead, try a chicken plank which has only

9 carbs. It's even batter dipped for an extra treat.
- Shrimp Sauce and Tartar Sauce have 3 carb grams per serving, while Malt Vinegar has 0.
- An order of Cheese Sticks has 12 grams of carbs. This can be confusing, because cheese products are usually excellent low carb choices. Compare it to a breaded Hush Puppy, a "high carb" food, with only 9 carbs.

**Every Carb Counts**

You do have to "sweat the small stuff" when it comes to losing weight. Even salad dressings can be tricky. For example, Wendy's Fat Free French is 19 carbs. Their regular Blue Cheese dressing is only 3 carbs. In between those two choices lie the 11 gram Honey Mustard and the 6 gram Creamy Ranch. Those differences in numbers do add up. There are big differences in soft drinks too. A small regular cola or Sprite has 40 carbs and a giant diet drink has zero.

**Create Your Own Personal List**
When you are ready to begin a low carb diet, be prepared. Your best bet is to spend some time with the **Carb Chart™**. Take time to locate your usual menu picks from your favorite restaurants and see how they add up. If these items won't fit into your

new eating style, search for other choices to replace them. Additional low carb choices are added to restaurant menus on a frequent basis. Make regular visits to *www.LowCarbFastFoodDiet.com* for the newest menu items, free downloads, and the folding pocket-sized **Carb-Chart** $^{TM}$ (folds up to the size of a credit card).

# Chapter Four:
## What Your Body Wants You to Know

The *concept* of dieting is great. You dream of a total body transformation and a closet full of new clothes in smaller sizes. You are excited that you will be healthier than ever and somehow magically sculpted and toned. You are eager to start dropping pounds and living in that transformed body.

The *process* of dieting may not be so wonderful. You come home from work or school and reach for your usual snack without thinking. You might have it in your hands, unwrapping it, before it dawns on you…oops! You are supposed to be dieting. Remember that commitment you made to change your habits and your lifestyle? Well, it was supposed to be *today*.

So, how do you stick to a diet plan when you're not inclined to do so? Is it possible for a person who has never succeeded in dieting to stay on a low carb program long enough to lose weight?

The answer is yes! It is possible. And it doesn't have to be difficult. It will, however, involve change. The change is this: alter your thinking. But change does not have to be unpleasant. *The Low Carb Fast Food Diet* helps you become nutritionally aware and look at fast food in a new way. You can love your fast food again! Be proud to declare your affection, but be prepared to make that change in your thinking.

### Lifestyle Evaluation: Are You Ready for Change?

Place a check mark next to the statements that apply to you.

○ I have failed on other diets.

○ I don't think I can stay on a diet.

○ I don't really want to diet, but I know I should for my health.

○ I believe all fast foods are bad for you.

○ I don't like change.

○ I believe I can lose weight by eating the right fast foods.

Did you mark any of those statements? If so, here are a few tips to help you transform your mindset and encourage your good habits.

**Love Yourself, Not Your Buns**
Love your fast food but don't love your buns. Hamburger buns (at approximately 30 carbs), hotdog buns, sandwich bread - you get the idea. On *The Low Carb Fast Food Diet*, you will avoid those buns like a carbohydrate plague. They are high in carbs and low in fiber. That means they should be the first item to remove from your food intake. Yet, bun-avoidance is not the only trick to this diet.

**Got Dairy?**
Calcium helps you to lose weight. Experts say that dieters who consumed calcium (at 1100 mg a day) in dairy products like yogurt lost an amazing 22% more weight than dieters taking only 500 mg of the nutrient while eating the same foods. Now there are multiple low carb flavors of yogurt available and, of course, calcium supplements as well. Dairy also includes vitamin D which aids the body in absorbing calcium. Moreover, it provides protein, B vitamins, magnesium and phosphorus for bones.

**In With the Fiber, Out With... Everything Else**
Fiber is a diet superstar too often ignored. It makes you feel full faster, and this helps you consume fewer carbs/calories. Fiber moves food quickly through your intestines and aids with the removal of fat. It is essential for digestive health and may

lower cancer risk. To avoid carbs or calories, supplement your fiber intake with a sugar-free fiber product.

**Something Smells Fishy**
Tuna fish and salmon both contain omega-3 fatty acids which have been linked to lowered risk of heart disease. Further, omega-3 is reported to relieve inflammation in the body.

**Your Cup Should Runneth Over**
Water does far more than hydrate us. It carries nutrients to every nook and cranny of the body. Drinking enough water (a minimum of 6 to 8 glasses per day) helps improve metabolism. It can decrease appetite because, without enough liquids, you may think you are craving food, when you actually need water.

**Tea Time**
Green and black teas have been linked to increased weight loss. Also, both are loaded with antioxidants that prevent heart disease, cancer, osteoporosis and stroke. So, order iced or hot tea instead of diet soda, if you are not having water.

**Let Them Eat Lettuce**
This wonderful, leafy veggie has almost no carbs and only 3 to 5 calories per ½ cup serving. Lettuce is versatile, yet loaded with vitamin A and the heart-helper vitamin B folate. This translates into added

protection from cancer and heart disease. Stick to dark green lettuce to reap the most health benefits.

**"Heap the onions, please"**
Don't let those onions pass you by. Low in carbs and calories, they are also high in the vitamin B folate and vitamin C. Scallions contain small amounts of vitamin A from the green chlorophyll. Onions can add lots of flavor to your diet. Just make sure the onions you select are *not* of the fried onion ring variety.
.

**Low Carb Makes You Nuts**
Recently, the FDA approved the first health claim for a food stating that eating 1 ½ ounces of most nuts each day may reduce heart disease risk. A low carb food, nuts are a health superstar, full of unsaturated fat, magnesium, vitamin E and folate. So go nuts with almonds, walnuts, peanuts and pistachios. When getting gasoline, you can make a quick pass at the snack counter and actually come back with something that will improve your health and help keep the carbs down.

**Vegetable or Fruit… Who Cares?**
Tomatoes are low carb and low calorie, but sky high nutritionally. At less than 5 carbs and 25 calories for a medium tomato, they pack in folate, vitamin A and potassium. This fruit helps fight prostate cancer with the nutrient lycopene, and a 1997 European study showed fewer heart attacks among men eating tomatoes.

**Fork Your Pizza**

Up to half of all Americans eat pizza once a week. If you indulge, ditch the crust. The gooey surface pulls right off providing you with all of the flavor and none of the fattening crust. A crispy vegetable topping provides vitamins and cancer-fighting lycopene piled on a dish not traditionally known for wholesome goodness.

**Sweet Indulgence**

Chocolate is arguably the world's favorite confection. If you just have to have it, go for one ounce dark chocolate, not milk chocolate. Happily, the dark version will not provide empty carbs. It contains flavonoids and catechins, the same chemicals that make tea and red wine heart-healthy.

**Down With Vitamins**

Last but not least, take a multi-vitamin and mineral supplement each day. When dieting, it is even more important. Vitamins are essentially organic substances that are not produced by the body (except vitamin D). Therefore, you must get them from either food or dietary supplements.

**You Know It's True**

Muscle burns fat; exercise builds muscle. So, start exercising. Begin with walking and start slowly to build stamina. It won't take long before you see a slimmer, fitter body in that full-length mirror. Your doctor can advise you on the best way to begin an exercise routine.

**Nighttime Cravings**
The urge for a bedtime snack is more habitual than chemical. The best way to beat those late night cravings is to outsmart them. Help your taste buds fall asleep with this simple strategy. Brush, floss and use a strong, long-lasting mouthwash. Top that fresh sensation off with a product such as Listerine breath strips. Repeat as necessary. Before you know it, you won't be able to taste your mom's apple pie - real or imaginary.

The hints listed in this chapter are not the only helpful weight loss tips out there. As you persist with your plan, you'll find your own useful techniques. All of them will help you stay motivated and give you more energy, better health and fewer pounds. If ever there was a program for the motivationally challenged, this is it.

# Chapter Five:
# For Calorie Counters Everywhere

We used to count calories, every single calorie that crossed our lips. Some of you still have calorie values memorized. And as much as we despised the rigid system, calorie counting did provide us an opportunity to indulge. A small apple or a bite of rich chocolate cake both have ninety calories. To chocolate lovers, the choice was simple.

The low calorie weight loss tradition has worked for millions, been prescribed by doctors for decades and has withstood the scrutiny of multitudes of studies. You may have friends, a spouse or a family member that prefers counting calories to carbs. This chapter is for them.

Before beginning a low calorie diet, remember that any eating plan that causes you to starve yourself is not a healthy approach. Food is NOT your enemy. That means you need to eat, and eat well. Do not cut down your food intake to so few calories that you are often hungry or even starving. Understanding the strategy behind low calorie eating will help you decide how much to eat. So, here is the real number crunch that you will need to do for your daily calorie intake.

**You Do the Math**
Right now, if you are an average American, you take in 2500 to 3500 calories per day. (Men consume on the high end of that range.) The magic number for low calorie weight loss is 3500. That is the amount of calories it takes to add or subtract one pound of body fat.

If you eliminate 500 calories per day for 7 days, for example, you should lose one pound in one week.

If you typically eat 2500 calories a day, and you drop down to a 1500 calorie diet, then you will save yourself 1000 calories every 24 hours. Multiply that number (1000) x 7 days, and you will save 7000 calories in a week. At 3500 calories per pound, that is a weight loss of 2 pounds a week.

It isn't difficult to do. The meal suggestions in this chapter weigh in at a three meal daily total of approximately 1300 – 1500 calories. When you do the math, you could lose approximately 2 pounds a week while eating convenient and varied fast food meals. No points, no contracts, no special meal purchases. Plus, low calorie drive-thru meals are amazingly plentiful, if you know what to order.

**Get the Facts on Your Eating**
To make it easy for those of you who count calories, these counts are included in the **Carb Chart™** as well. Just as with carbohydrates, studies show that most people are not aware of the total number of calories they consume in a day. The **Carb Chart™** can save you from becoming one more dieting casualty, steering you away from calorie blunders.

For instance:

- An Auntie Anne's Glazin' Raisin Pretzel seems relatively healthy, but it weighs in at a total of 510 calories. Compare that to Auntie Anne's Almond Pretzel without butter, for a savings of nearly 200 calories.

- Most muffins are simply cake in a single serving. Many muffins, like bran or whole grain, might sound like a dieter's dream, but they're actually a hefty 400+ calories. That mistake could, instead, give you nightmares.

- A friendly coffeehouse chat could turn into a raging war against your transforming body, since a 16 ounce Dunkin' Donuts Coffee Coolotta with milk has 210 calories. Not bad for an indulgent, frothy drink, but don't add a bagel. Your combo would then rank a whopping 550+ calories. As harsh as these examples might seem, brace yourself for another shock.

## Your Waistline May Be Attacked by Your Next Salad

One serving of the Taco Salad at Taco Bell contains a whopping 790 calories and 42 grams of fat. You could order it without the shell, but it still rings in at 420 calories and 21 grams of fat. After this bad news, you may feel discouraged. But cheer up. Over the next few pages, you will see a wide variety of choices, all low calorie, all easily ordered and all prepared by someone else. With this information, you have several different choices for each meal every day of the week.

Once you are familiar with the **Carb Chart™**, you will discover other meal combinations. *Just remember these meals are based on calories, not carbs*, so limit your total daily intake to fall within your personal calorie range.

Take a look at some choices for your next week.

# LOW CALORIE Meal Choices
## LUNCH

| McDonald's | KFC | Boston Market |
|---|---|---|
| Chicken Mc Grill<br>Side Salad<br>Light Italian<br>Dressing<br>Fruit and Yogurt<br>Parfait<br>Bottled Water<br>537 cal | Honey BBQ<br>Sandwich<br>Mashed<br>Potatoes<br>Gravy<br>Green Beans<br>Iced Tea<br>463 cal | Rotisserie<br>Turkey<br>Green Beans<br>Vegetable<br>Medley<br>Bottled Water<br>260 cal |
| **Wendy's** | **McDonald's** | **KFC** |
| Small Chili<br>Baked Potato<br>1 Packet<br>Country Crock<br>Diet Drink<br><br>540 cal | Hamburger<br>Small French<br>Fries<br>Bottled Water<br><br><br>490 cal | Chicken Breast<br>w/o Skin<br>Baked Beans<br>Diet Drink<br><br><br>370 cal |
| **Taco Bell** | **Boston Market** | **McDonald's** |
| Fresco Soft Taco<br>with Grilled<br>Steak<br>Mexican Rice<br>Diet Drink<br><br><br><br>500 cal | Honey Glazed<br>Ham<br>Vegetable<br>Medley<br>Caesar Side<br>Salad<br>(no croutons)<br>Bottled Water<br>470 cal | 6 Chicken<br>Nuggets<br>BBQ Sauce<br>Side Salad<br>Low Fat<br>Balsamic<br>Vinaigrette<br>Dressing<br>340 cal |

# <u>LOW CALORIE</u> Meal Choices
## DINNER

| Taco Bell | Burger King | McDonald's |
|---|---|---|
| Fresco Fiesta Burrito with Chicken Pintos n' Cheese Diet Drink<br><br>480 cal | Shrimp Caesar Salad Fat Free Ranch Dressing Iced Tea<br><br><br>215 cal | Grilled Chicken California Cobb Newman's Own Low Fat Balsamic Vinaigrette Dressing Vanilla Reduced Fat Ice Cream Cone<br>460 cal |
| **Wendy's** | **McDonald's** | **Taco Bell** |
| Mandarin Chicken Salad Low-fat Honey Mustard Dressing Iced Tea<br><br>490 cal | Grilled Chicken Caesar Salad Newman's Own Low Fat Balsamic Vinaigrette Dressing Bottled Water<br>240 cal | Gordita Supreme with Chicken Mexican Rice Diet Drink<br><br><br>490 cal |
| **McDonald's** | **Burger King** | **Boston Market** |
| Regular Cheeseburger Vanilla Reduced Fat Ice Cream Cone Bottled Water<br>480 cal | Veggie Burger Reduced Fat Mayo Small Onion Rings Diet Drink<br><br>520 cal | ¼ Rotisserie Chicken (no skin or wing) Vegetable Medley Fruit Salad Bottled Water<br>380 cal |

If you keep on track with low calorie meals and continue to do the same amount of physical activity, one to two pounds a week should be an attainable goal. Once you establish your new eating routine, gradually increase your daily exercise. Along with new eating habits, this will help you lose even more.

**Fast Food Snack Attack - *Remember, this section is for low-calorie dieters ONLY!***
You might have cravings when you're on the go. If your three daily meals stay under the 1300-1500 daily calorie range (this goal varies according to gender, age, and body type), here are a few occasional splurges for a special treat. Each is approximately 300 calories.

McDonald's Apple Pie
Subway Cookie
Wendy's Plain Baked Potato
KFC Cherry Cheesecake Parfait
Wendy's Junior Frosty
BK Hershey's Sundae Pie
Dunkin' Donuts Apple, Cheese or Cherry Danish
KFC Apple Pie
Six Subway Fruit Roll-ups

Some items that sound like diet danger are actually fine for low calorie eating. You will want to keep the **Carb Chart™** with you to check calories on any menu item that is not familiar to you. Remember, do not assume you know a value. Better to take a quick look and stay with the right low calorie foods.

# Part Two

# How to Use the Carb Chart™

You are holding the key to diet success in your hands - the **Carb Chart™**. Keep a copy in your car, gym bag, purse or briefcase for those unexpected trips through the drive-thru. Now all those choices, confusing menu charts and nutrition terms become simple.

How do you know what to order? It's easy.

- The **Carb Chart™** is set up alphabetically from Arby's to Wendy's.
- Under each restaurant section, you will find carbohydrate counts, net carbs* (where applicable), calories, fat, fiber, sodium and cholesterol for hundreds of menu selections.
- Drink Choices: General information for soft drinks, coffee, tea and juices are listed in the final section.

*Net Carbs - The Net Carb is a term coined by the Atkins program. It is calculated as the total carbohydrate count of a food minus the number of fiber grams. In the case of controlled-carb products sweetened with glycerin or sugar alcohols, those are subtracted as well.

---

*Note*: Brands are trademarks of their respective holders and menu items and nutrient values are subject to change without notice. Nutrient values are listed unless unavailable at the time of publication, and variations in values can be due to local and distribution factors, and errors and omissions can occur. All questions regarding values found in the **Carb Chart™** should be directed to the individual restaurant. This is intended as a general guide only for nutritional content of popular restaurant menu items.

# ARBY'S

| | Size | Carb (g) | Cal. (g) | Fiber (g) | Total Chol. (mg) | Fat (g) | Sod. (mg) |
|---|---|---|---|---|---|---|---|
| **Roast Beef Sandwiches** | | | | | | | |
| Arby-Q | 1 | 51 | 360 | 2 | 35 | 11 | 1210 |
| Beef n' Cheddar | 1 | 44 | 440 | 2 | 50 | 21 | 1270 |
| Big Montana | 1 | 41 | 590 | 3 | 115 | 29 | 2080 |
| Giant Roast Beef | 1 | 41 | 450 | 2 | 75 | 19 | 1440 |
| Junior Roast Beef | 1 | 34 | 270 | 2 | 30 | 9 | 740 |
| Regular Roast Beef | 1 | 34 | 320 | 2 | 45 | 13 | 950 |
| Super Roast Beef | 1 | 48 | 440 | 3 | 45 | 19 | 1130 |
| **Sandwiches** | | | | | | | |
| Chicken Bacon n' Swiss | 1 | 49 | 550 | 2 | 70 | 27 | 1640 |
| Chicken Breast Filet | 1 | 46 | 490 | 2 | 55 | 24 | 1220 |
| Chicken Cordon Bleu | 1 | 46 | 570 | 2 | 85 | 29 | 1880 |
| Grilled Chicken Deluxe | 1 | 40 | 380 | 2 | 50 | 12 | 920 |

# ARBY'S – *continued*

## Sandwiches - *cont.*

| | Size | Carb (g) | Cal. (g) | Fiber (g) | Total Chol. (mg) | Fat (g) | Sod. (mg) |
|---|---|---|---|---|---|---|---|
| **Market Fresh Sandwiches & Wraps** | | | | | | | |
| Roast Beef and Swiss | 1 | 74 | 780 | 6 | 90 | 39 | 1740 |
| Roast Ham and Swiss | 1 | 74 | 700 | 5 | 85 | 31 | 2140 |
| Roast Turkey and Swiss | 1 | 74 | 720 | 5 | 90 | 27 | 1790 |
| Low Carby's Ultimate BLT Wrap - **17 net carbs** | 1 | 48 | 650 | 31 | 50 | 47 | 1730 |
| Low Carby's Southwest Chicken Wrap - **15 net carbs** | 1 | 45 | 550 | 30 | 75 | 30 | 1690 |
| Low Carby's Chicken Caesar Wrap - **16 net carbs** | 1 | 46 | 520 | 30 | 65 | 27 | 1530 |
| **Market Fresh Salads** | | | | | | | |
| Asian Sesame Salad- no dressing | 1 | 15 | 140 | 3 | 40 | 1 | 360 |

# ARBY'S – *continued*

## Market Fresh Salads – *cont.*

| | Size | Carb (g) | Cal. (g) | Fiber (g) | Total Chol. (mg) | Fat (g) | Sod. (mg) |
|---|---|---|---|---|---|---|---|
| Martha's Vineyard Salad- no dressing | 1 | 23 | 250 | 4 | 60 | 8 | 490 |
| Santa Fe Salad- no dressing | 1 | 40 | 520 | 5 | 60 | 29 | 1120 |
| Garden Side Salad | 1 | 7 | 35 | 5 | 0 | 0 | 25 |

## Dressings

| | Size | Carb (g) | Cal. (g) | Fiber (g) | Total Chol. (mg) | Fat (g) | Sod. (mg) |
|---|---|---|---|---|---|---|---|
| Light Balsamic Vinaigrette | 1 | 13 | 110 | 0 | 0 | 6 | 220 |
| Buttermilk Ranch | 1 | 3 | 290 | 0 | 25 | 30 | 580 |
| Buttermilk Ranch, Reduced Calorie | 1 | 12 | 100 | 1 | 0 | 6 | 486 |
| Santa Fe Ranch | 1 | 3 | 264 | 0 | 19 | 28 | 615 |
| Italian, Reduced Calorie | 1 | 7 | 30 | 0 | 0 | 0 | 520 |
| Asian Sesame | 1 | 15 | 190 | 0 | 0 | 14 | 463 |

## Sides

| | Size | Carb (g) | Cal. (g) | Fiber (g) | Total Chol. (mg) | Fat (g) | Sod. (mg) |
|---|---|---|---|---|---|---|---|
| Chicken Finger Snack (2) | 1 | 53 | 590 | 3 | 35 | 34 | 1430 |
| Chicken Finger 4-Pack | 1 | 42 | 640 | 3 | 70 | 38 | 1590 |

**ARBY'S** – *continued*

**Sides** – *cont.*

| | Size | Carb (g) | Cal. (g) | Fiber (g) | Total Chol. (mg) | Fat (g) | Sod. (mg) |
|---|---|---|---|---|---|---|---|
| Cheddar Cheese Sauce | 1 | 4 | 60 | 0 | 0 | 4.5 | 360 |
| Curly Fries | Sm | 39 | 340 | 4 | 0 | 18 | 790 |
| Curly Fries | Md | 47 | 410 | 5 | 0 | 22 | 950 |
| Curly Fries | Lg | 73 | 630 | 7 | 0 | 34 | 1480 |
| Homestyle Fries | Sm | 44 | 300 | 3 | 0 | 13 | 550 |
| Homestyle Fries | Md | 55 | 380 | 4 | 0 | 16 | 690 |
| Homestyle Fries | Lg | 82 | 570 | 6 | 0 | 24 | 1030 |
| Potato Cakes | 2 | 26 | 250 | 2 | 0 | 15 | 390 |
| Broccoli N' Cheddar Baked Potato | 1 | 56 | 460 | 6 | 50 | 23 | 780 |
| Jalapeno Bites | 5 | 30 | 330 | 2 | 40 | 21 | 530 |
| Mozzarella Sticks | 4 | 38 | 430 | 2 | 45 | 23 | 1370 |
| Onion Petals | Reg | 35 | 330 | 2 | 0 | 19 | 330 |
| **Breakfast** | | | | | | | |
| Biscuit with Ham | 1 | 27 | 270 | <1 | 20 | 13 | 1170 |

# ARBY'S – *continued*

## Breakfast - *cont.*

| | Size | Carb (g) | Cal. (g) | Fiber (g) | Total Chol. (mg) | Fat (g) | Sod. (mg) |
|---|---|---|---|---|---|---|---|
| Biscuit with Sausage | 1 | 26 | 390 | <1 | 30 | 27 | 1080 |
| Biscuit with Bacon | 1 | 27 | 300 | <1 | 15 | 17 | 950 |
| Croissant with Ham n' Cheese | 1 | 30 | 350 | <1 | 65 | 19 | 870 |
| Croissant with Sausage n' Egg | 1 | 31 | 510 | <1 | 210 | 36 | 800 |
| Croissant with Bacon n' Egg | 1 | 31 | 410 | <1 | 190 | 26 | 670 |
| Sourdough with Ham, Egg & Swiss | 1 | 33 | 450 | 1 | 330 | 23 | 1750 |
| Sourdough with Egg & Cheese | 1 | 31 | 330 | 1 | 165 | 16 | 1060 |
| Sourdough with Bacon, Egg & Swiss | 1 | 33 | 500 | 1 | 325 | 29 | 1600 |

## BOSTON MARKET

| | Size | Carb (g) | Cal. (g) | Fiber (g) | Total Chol. (mg) | Fat (g) | Sod. (mg) |
|---|---|---|---|---|---|---|---|
| **Entrees** | | | | | | | |
| 1/2 Rotisserie Chicken | 1 | 4 | 590 | 0 | 290 | 33 | 1010 |
| 1/4 Rotisserie Chicken Dark | 1 | 2 | 320 | 0 | 155 | 21 | 500 |
| 1/4 Rotisserie Chicken- Dark no skin | 1 | 1 | 190 | 0 | 115 | 10 | 440 |
| 1/4 Rotisserie Chicken- White | 1 | 2 | 280 | 0 | 135 | 12 | 510 |
| 1/4 Rotisserie Chicken- White no skin | 1 | 2 | 170 | 0 | 85 | 4 | 480 |
| Crispy Baked Chicken | 1 | 31 | 420 | 5 | 35 | 22 | 880 |
| Grilled Marinated Chicken | 1 | 1 | 230 | 0 | 90 | 10 | 220 |
| Grilled Mango Chicken | 1 | 26 | 390 | 0 | 145 | 12 | 930 |
| Honey Glazed Ham | 1 | 10 | 210 | 0 | 75 | 8 | 1460 |

# BOSTON MARKET - *continued*

## Entrees - *cont.*

| | Size | Carb (g) | Cal. (g) | Fiber (g) | Total Chol. (mg) | Fat (g) | Sod. (mg) |
|---|---|---|---|---|---|---|---|
| Meatloaf | 1 | 16 | 310 | 1 | 75 | 19 | 650 |
| Meatloaf w/ Creole Sauce | 1 | 25 | 350 | 2 | 75 | 19 | 1020 |
| Meatloaf w/ Gravy | 1 | 19 | 360 | 1 | 75 | 23 | 920 |
| North Atlantic Cod | 1 | 11 | 320 | 0 | 130 | 15 | 410 |
| Rotisserie Turkey | 1 | 3 | 170 | 0 | 100 | 1 | 850 |

## Sides

| | Size | Carb (g) | Cal. (g) | Fiber (g) | Total Chol. (mg) | Fat (g) | Sod. (mg) |
|---|---|---|---|---|---|---|---|
| Cornbread | 1 | 33 | 200 | 1 | 25 | 6 | 390 |
| Butternut Squash | 1 | 25 | 150 | 6 | 20 | 6 | 560 |
| Sweet Corn | 1 | 30 | 180 | 2 | 0 | 4 | 170 |
| Creamed Spinach | 1 | 11 | 260 | 2 | 55 | 20 | 740 |
| Green Beans | 1 | 6 | 70 | 2 | 0 | 4 | 250 |
| Green Bean Casserole | 1 | 9 | 80 | 2 | 5 | 5 | 670 |
| Cinnamon Apples | 1 | 56 | 250 | 3 | 0 | 5 | 45 |
| Macaroni and Cheese | 1 | 33 | 280 | 1 | 30 | 11 | 890 |
| Mashed Potatoes | 1 | 30 | 210 | 2 | 25 | 9 | 590 |

# BOSTON MARKET - *continued*

## Sides – *cont.*

| | Size | Carb (g) | Cal. (g) | Fiber (g) | Total Chol. (mg) | Fat (g) | Sod. (mg) |
|---|---|---|---|---|---|---|---|
| Mashed Potatoes with Gravy | 1 | 32 | 230 | 3 | 25 | 9 | 780 |
| Garlic Dill New Potatoes | 1 | 25 | 130 | 2 | 0 | 3 | 150 |
| Vegetable Rice Pilaf | 1 | 24 | 140 | 1 | 0 | 4 | 520 |
| Stuffing | 1 | 27 | 190 | 2 | 5 | 8 | 620 |
| Sweet Potato Casserole | 1 | 39 | 280 | 2 | 10 | 13 | 190 |
| Steamed Vegetable Medley | 1 | 6 | 30 | 2 | 0 | 0 | 135 |
| Squash Casserole | 1 | 20 | 330 | 3 | 70 | 24 | 1110 |
| Tomato Au Gratin | 1 | 14 | 160 | 1 | 15 | 10 | 1240 |
| **Soup and Salad** | | | | | | | |
| Caesar Side Salad | 1 | 13 | 300 | 1 | 15 | 26 | 690 |
| Caesar Salad Entrée | 1 | 17 | 470 | 3 | 35 | 40 | 1070 |
| Grilled Chicken Caesar Salad | 1 | 18 | 800 | 3 | 140 | 62 | 1770 |

## BOSTON MARKET - *continued*

## Soup & Salad – *cont.*

| | Size | Carb (g) | Cal. (g) | Fiber (g) | Total Chol. (mg) | Fat (g) | Sod. (mg) |
|---|---|---|---|---|---|---|---|
| Southwest Grilled Chicken salad | 1 | 46 | 890 | 7 | 115 | 58 | 1100 |
| Southwest Grilled Chicken Salad- no dressing or chips | 1 | 22 | 470 | 6 | 115 | 23 | 480 |
| Oriental Grilled Chicken Salad | 1 | 56 | 570 | 8 | 95 | 20 | 1770 |
| Oriental Grilled Chicken Salad- no dressing or noodles | 1 | 21 | 300 | 7 | 95 | 9 | 440 |
| Coleslaw | 1 | 29 | 310 | 10 | 20 | 22 | 230 |
| Fruit Salad | 1 | 16 | 70 | 1 | 0 | 0 | 15 |
| Tortilla Soup | 1 | 18 | 170 | 2 | 25 | 8 | 1060 |
| Tortilla Soup- no toppings | 1 | 7 | 80 | 1 | 15 | 5 | 930 |
| Chicken Noodle Soup | 1 | 8 | 100 | 0 | 30 | 5 | 500 |
| Tomato Bisque Soup | 1 | 25 | 380 | 4 | 65 | 29 | 1660 |
| 15 Vegetable Soup | 1 | 24 | 110 | 4 | 0 | 3 | 760 |

# BOSTON MARKET - *continued*

| | Size | Carb (g) | Cal. (g) | Fiber (g) | Total Chol. (mg) | Fat (g) | Sod. (mg) |
|---|---|---|---|---|---|---|---|
| **Dressings** | | | | | | | |
| Caesar | 60g | na | 290 | 0 | na | 31 | 680 |
| **Desserts** | | | | | | | |
| Apple Pie | 1 | 66 | 550 | 3 | 0 | 31 | 240 |
| Caramel Pecan Brownie | 1 | 114 | 900 | 6 | 120 | 47 | 150 |
| Chocolate Brownie | 1 | 88 | 580 | 6 | 95 | 23 | 350 |
| Chocolate Cake | 1 | 86 | 650 | 2 | 60 | 32 | 320 |
| Chocolate Chip Cookie | 1 | 51 | 390 | 2 | 15 | 19 | 350 |
| Chocolate Mania | 1 | 36 | 490 | 1 | 95 | 33 | 170 |
| Oatmeal Scotchie Cookie | 1 | 47 | 390 | 2 | 30 | 20 | 340 |

# BURGER KING

| | Size | Carb (g) | Cal. (g) | Fiber (g) | Total Chol. (mg) | Fat (g) | Sod. (mg) |
|---|---|---|---|---|---|---|---|
| **Burgers** | | | | | | | |
| Bacon Cheeseburger | 1 | 31 | 390 | 1 | 60 | 20 | 990 |
| Bacon Double Cheeseburger | 1 | 32 | 570 | 2 | 110 | 34 | 1250 |
| Cheeseburger | 1 | 31 | 350 | 1 | 50 | 17 | 770 |
| Double Cheeseburger | 1 | 32 | 530 | 2 | 100 | 31 | 1030 |
| Hamburger | 1 | 31 | 310 | 1 | 40 | 13 | 550 |
| Double Hamburger | 1 | 30 | 440 | 1 | 75 | 23 | 600 |
| Whopper | 1 | 52 | 700 | 4 | 85 | 42 | 1020 |
| Whopper with Cheese | 1 | 53 | 800 | 4 | 110 | 49 | 1450 |
| Double Whopper | 1 | 52 | 970 | 4 | 160 | 61 | 1110 |
| Double Whopper with Cheese | 1 | 53 | 1060 | 4 | 185 | 69 | 1540 |
| Whopper Jr. | 1 | 31 | 390 | 2 | 45 | 22 | 550 |
| Veggie Burger | 1 | 46 | 380 | 4 | 5 | 16 | 930 |
| Low Carb Angus Steak | 1 | 5 | 350 | <1 | 75 | 28 | 630 |

## BURGER KING - *continued*

### Burgers – *cont.*

|  | Size | Carb (g) | Cal. (g) | Fiber (g) | Total Chol. (mg) | Fat (g) | Sod. (mg) |
|---|---|---|---|---|---|---|---|
| Low Carb Angus Steak w/ Bacon Cheese | 1 | 7 | 500 | 1 | 105 | 40 | 1350 |
| Angus Steak | 1 | 62 | 640 | 3 | 75 | 32 | 1170 |
| Angus Steak w/ Bacon & Cheese | 1 | 64 | 790 | 3 | 105 | 44 | 1890 |

### Sandwiches

|  | Size | Carb (g) | Cal. (g) | Fiber (g) | Total Chol. (mg) | Fat (g) | Sod. (mg) |
|---|---|---|---|---|---|---|---|
| Chicken Sandwich | 1 | 52 | 560 | 3 | 60 | 28 | 1270 |
| Chicken Whopper | 1 | 48 | 580 | 4 | 75 | 26 | 1370 |
| Fish Filet | 1 | 44 | 520 | 2 | 55 | 30 | 840 |

### Salads, Specialties and Sides

|  | Size | Carb (g) | Cal. (g) | Fiber (g) | Total Chol. (mg) | Fat (g) | Sod. (mg) |
|---|---|---|---|---|---|---|---|
| Chicken Caesar Salad w/o Dressing | 1 | 9 | 190 | 1 | 50 | 7 | 900 |
| Chicken Caesar Salad w/ Creamy Garlic Caesar Dressing | 1 | 17 | 330 | 2 | 65 | 18 | 1610 |
| Side Garden Salad- w/o dressing | 1 | 5 | 25 | 2 | 0 | 0 | 15 |
| Chicken Tenders | 5 | 13 | 210 | <1 | 30 | 12 | 530 |

## BURGER KING – *continued*

## Salads, Specialties & Sides – *cont.*

| | Size | Carb (g) | Cal. (g) | Fiber (g) | Total Chol.( mg) | Fat (g) | Sod. (mg) |
|---|---|---|---|---|---|---|---|
| Chili | 1 | 17 | 190 | 5 | 25 | 8 | 1040 |
| French Fries | Sm | 29 | 230 | 2 | 0 | 11 | 410 |
| French Fries | Lg | 63 | 500 | 5 | 0 | 25 | 880 |
| Onion Rings | Sm | 22 | 180 | 2 | 0 | 9 | 260 |
| Onion Rings | Lg | 60 | 480 | 5 | <5 | 23 | 690 |
| **Dressings** | | | | | | | |
| Sweet Onion Vinaigrette | 1 | 8 | 100 | 0 | 0 | 8 | 960 |
| Fat Free Ranch | 1 | 7 | 35 | 0 | 0 | 0 | 370 |
| Ranch | 1 | 7 | 120 | 0 | 20 | 10 | 610 |
| Tomato Balsamic Vinaigrette | 1 | 9 | 110 | 0 | 0 | 9 | 760 |
| Creamy Caesar | 1 | 7 | 130 | 0 | 20 | 11 | 710 |
| **Desserts** | | | | | | | |
| Dutch Apple Pie | 1 | 52 | 340 | 1 | 0 | 14 | 470 |
| Hershey's Sundae Pie | 1 | 31 | 300 | 1 | 10 | 18 | 190 |

# BURGER KING – *continued*

## Desserts – *cont.*

| | Size | Carb (g) | Cal. (g) | Fiber (g) | Total Chol.( mg) | Fat (g) | Sod. (mg) |
|---|---|---|---|---|---|---|---|
| Nestle Toll House Cookies | 2 | 68 | 440 | 0 | 20 | 16 | 360 |
| Vanilla Shake | Sm | 57 | 400 | 0 | 60 | 15 | 240 |
| Vanilla Shake | Md | 76 | 540 | 0 | 80 | 20 | 320 |
| Chocolate Shake | Sm | 65 | 410 | 0 | 50 | 13 | 300 |
| Chocolate Shake | Md | 97 | 600 | 2 | 70 | 18 | 470 |
| Strawberry Shake | Sm | 64 | 410 | 0 | 50 | 13 | 220 |
| Strawberry Shake | Md | 96 | 590 | 0 | 70 | 17 | 300 |
| **Breakfast** | | | | | | | |
| Croissanwich Bacon/Egg/ Chz | 1 | 25 | 360 | <1 | 195 | 22 | 950 |
| Croissanwich Egg/Chz | 1 | 24 | 320 | <1 | 185 | 19 | 730 |
| Croissanwich Ham/Egg/Chz | 1 | 25 | 360 | <1 | 200 | 20 | 1500 |
| Croissanwich Sausage/Egg/Chz | 1 | 24 | 520 | 1 | 210 | 39 | 1090 |
| French Toast Sticks | 5 | 46 | 390 | 2 | 0 | 20 | 440 |

# CHICK-FIL-A

| | Size | Carb (g) | Cal. (g) | Fiber (g) | Total Chol. (mg) | Fat (g) | Sod. (mg) |
|---|---|---|---|---|---|---|---|
| **Sandwiches** | | | | | | | |
| Chicken Sandwich | 1 | 38 | 410 | 1 | 60 | 16 | 1300 |
| Deluxe Chicken Sandwich | 1 | 39 | 420 | 2 | 60 | 16 | 1300 |
| Chicken Salad Sandwich | 1 | 32 | 350 | 5 | 65 | 15 | 880 |
| Chicken Only, no bun | 1 | 10 | 230 | 0 | 60 | 11 | 990 |
| Chargrilled Chicken Sandwich | 1 | 33 | 270 | 3 | 65 | 3.5 | 940 |
| Chargrilled Chicken Only, no bun | 1 | 1 | 100 | 0 | 65 | 1.5 | 610 |
| Chargrilled Chicken Club Sandwich (no sauce) | 1 | 33 | 380 | 3 | 90 | 11 | 1240 |
| **Cool Wraps** | | | | | | | |
| Chargrilled Chicken | 1 | 54 | 390 | 3 | 65 | 7 | 1020 |
| Chicken Caesar | 1 | 52 | 460 | 3 | 80 | 10 | 1350 |
| Spicy Chicken | 1 | 52 | 380 | 3 | 60 | 6 | 1090 |

# CHICK-FIL-A - *continued*

| | Size | Carb (g) | Cal. (g) | Fiber (g) | Total Chol. (mg) | Fat (g) | Sod. (mg) |
|---|---|---|---|---|---|---|---|
| **Specialties** | | | | | | | |
| Chick-N-Strips | 4 | 14 | 290 | 1 | 65 | 13 | 730 |
| Nuggets | 8 | 12 | 260 | <1 | 70 | 12 | 1090 |
| Waffle Fries | Sm | 34 | 280 | 5 | 0 | 14 | 105 |
| Breast of Chicken Soup | Reg. | 18 | 140 | 1 | 25 | 4 | 900 |
| **Salads (*no dressing*)** | | | | | | | |
| Chargrilled Chicken Garden Salad | 1 | 9 | 180 | 3 | 65 | 6 | 620 |
| Southwest Chargrilled Salad | 1 | 17 | 240 | 5 | 60 | 8 | 770 |
| Chick-N-Strips Salad | 1 | 22 | 390 | 4 | 80 | 18 | 860 |
| Side Salad | 1 | 4 | 60 | 2 | 10 | 3 | 75 |
| Coleslaw | 1 | 17 | 260 | 2 | 25 | 21 | 220 |
| Carrot Raisin Salad | 1 | 28 | 170 | 2 | 10 | 6 | 110 |
| **Dressings** | | | | | | | |
| Caesar | 1 | 1 | 160 | 0 | 30 | 17 | 240 |

# CHICK-FIL-A - *continued*

## Dressings - *cont.*

| | Size | Carb (g) | Cal. (g) | Fiber (g) | Total Chol. (mg) | Fat (g) | Sod. (mg) |
|---|---|---|---|---|---|---|---|
| Reduced Fat Raspberry Vinaigrette | 1 | 15 | 80 | 0 | 0 | 2 | 190 |
| Bleu Cheese | 1 | 1 | 150 | 0 | 20 | 16 | 300 |
| Buttermilk Ranch | 1 | 1 | 160 | 0 | 5 | 16 | 270 |
| Spicy | 1 | 2 | 140 | 0 | 5 | 14 | 130 |
| Thousand Island | 1 | 5 | 150 | 0 | 10 | 14 | 250 |
| Light Italian | 1 | 2 | 15 | 0 | 0 | 1 | 570 |
| Fat Free Honey Mustard | 1 | 14 | 60 | 0 | 0 | 0 | 200 |

## Desserts

| | Size | Carb (g) | Cal. (g) | Fiber (g) | Total Chol. (mg) | Fat (g) | Sod. (mg) |
|---|---|---|---|---|---|---|---|
| IceDream | 1 | 38 | 230 | 0 | 25 | 6 | 100 |
| IceDream Cone | 1 | 28 | 160 | 0 | 15 | 4 | 80 |
| Lemon Pie | 1 | 51 | 320 | 3 | 110 | 10 | 220 |
| Fudge Nut Brownie | 1 | 45 | 330 | 2 | 20 | 15 | 210 |
| Cheesecake | 1 | 30 | 340 | 2 | 90 | 21 | 270 |

## CHICK-FIL-A - *continued*

| | Size | Carb (g) | Cal. (g) | Fiber (g) | Total Chol. (mg) | Fat (g) | Sod. (mg) |
|---|---|---|---|---|---|---|---|
| **Breakfast** | | | | | | | |
| Plain Biscuit | 1 | 38 | 260 | 1 | 0 | 11 | 670 |
| Hot Buttered Biscuit | 1 | 38 | 270 | 1 | 0 | 12 | 680 |
| Egg Biscuit | 1 | 38 | 340 | 1 | 245 | 16 | 740 |
| Egg, Cheese Biscuit | 1 | 38 | 390 | 1 | 260 | 21 | 960 |
| Bacon Biscuit | 1 | 38 | 300 | 1 | 5 | 14 | 780 |
| Bacon, Egg Biscuit | 1 | 38 | 390 | 1 | 250 | 20 | 860 |
| Bacon, Egg, Cheese Biscuit | 1 | 38 | 430 | 1 | 265 | 24 | 1070 |
| Biscuit and Gravy | 1 | 44 | 310 | 1 | 5 | 13 | 930 |
| Chicken Biscuit | 1 | 43 | 400 | 2 | 30 | 18 | 1200 |
| Chicken, Cheese Biscuit | 1 | 43 | 450 | 2 | 45 | 23 | 1430 |
| Sausage Biscuit | 1 | 42 | 410 | 1 | 20 | 23 | 740 |
| Sausage, Egg Biscuit | 1 | 43 | 500 | 1 | 265 | 29 | 810 |
| Sausage, Egg, Cheese Biscuit | 1 | 43 | 540 | 1 | 280 | 33 | 1030 |

**CHICK-FIL-A - *continued***

**Breakfast – *cont.***

| | Size | Carb (g) | Cal. (g) | Fiber (g) | Total Chol. (mg) | Fat (g) | Sod. (mg) |
|---|---|---|---|---|---|---|---|
| Danish | 1 | 63 | 430 | 2 | 25 | 17 | 160 |
| Hash Browns | 1 | 20 | 170 | 2 | 10 | 9 | 350 |

## DAIRY QUEEN

| | Size | Carb (g) | Cal. (g) | Fiber (g) | Total Chol. (mg) | Fat (g) | Sod. (mg) |
|---|---|---|---|---|---|---|---|
| **Burgers** | | | | | | | |
| Hamburger | 1 | 29 | 290 | 2 | 45 | 12 | 630 |
| Cheeseburger | 1 | 29 | 340 | 2 | 55 | 17 | 850 |
| Double Cheeseburger | 1 | 30 | 540 | 2 | 115 | 31 | 1130 |
| Bacon Double Cheeseburger | 1 | 31 | 610 | 2 | 130 | 36 | 1380 |
| Ultimate Burger | 1 | 29 | 670 | 2 | 135 | 43 | 1210 |
| **Salads** | | | | | | | |
| Crispy Chicken Salad, no dressing | 1 | 24 | 360 | 6 | 40 | 20 | 620 |
| Grilled Chicken Salad, no dressing | 1 | 12 | 240 | 4 | 65 | 10 | 950 |
| **Dressings** | | | | | | | |
| DQ Honey Mustard | | 18 | 260 | 0 | 20 | 21 | 370 |
| DQ Bleu Cheese Dressing | | 4 | 210 | 0 | 5 | 20 | 700 |
| DQ Ranch Dressing | | 3 | 310 | 0 | 25 | 33 | 390 |
| Reduced Calorie Buttermilk Dressing | | 5 | 140 | 0 | 15 | 13 | 390 |

# DAIRY QUEEN – *continued*

## Dressings – *cont.*

| | Size | Carb (g) | Cal. (g) | Fiber (g) | Total Chol. (mg) | Fat (g) | Sod. (mg) |
|---|---|---|---|---|---|---|---|
| Fat-Free Thousand Island | | 16 | 60 | 0 | 0 | 0 | 400 |
| Fat-Free Italian | | 3 | 10 | 0 | 0 | 0 | 390 |
| Wishbone Fat-Free Italian | | 6 | 25 | 0 | 0 | 0 | 520 |

## Specialties

| | Size | Carb (g) | Cal. (g) | Fiber (g) | Total Chol. (mg) | Fat (g) | Sod. (mg) |
|---|---|---|---|---|---|---|---|
| Chicken Strip Basket | 1 | 102 | 1000 | 5 | 55 | 50 | 2510 |
| Grilled Chicken Sandwich | 1 | 26 | 340 | 2 | 55 | 16 | 1000 |
| Hot Dog | 1 | 19 | 240 | 1 | 25 | 14 | 730 |
| Chili n' Cheese Dog | 1 | 22 | 330 | 2 | 45 | 21 | 1090 |
| French Fries | Sm | 45 | 300 | 3 | 0 | 12 | 700 |
| French Fries | Med | 56 | 380 | 4 | 0 | 15 | 880 |
| Onion Rings | 1 | 45 | 470 | 3 | 0 | 30 | 740 |

# DUNKIN' DONUTS

| | Size | Carb (g) | Cal. (g) | Fiber (g) | Total Chol. (mg) | Fat (g) | Sod. (mg) |
|---|---|---|---|---|---|---|---|
| **Bagels** | | | | | | | |
| Berry Berry | 1 | 69 | 340 | 4 | 0 | 3 | 540 |
| Blueberry | 1 | 69 | 350 | 2 | 0 | 3 | 630 |
| Cinnamon Raisin | 1 | 65 | 330 | 3 | 0 | 3 | 560 |
| Everything | 1 | 75 | 430 | 3 | 0 | 7 | 780 |
| Garlic | 1 | 79 | 410 | 3 | 0 | 3.5 | 790 |
| Onion | 1 | 71 | 370 | 4 | 0 | 4 | 650 |
| Plain | 1 | 69 | 360 | 2 | 0 | 3 | 780 |
| Poppyseed | 1 | 72 | 440 | 3 | 0 | 10 | 780 |
| Salt | 1 | 69 | 360 | 2 | 0 | 3 | 6590 |
| Sesame | 1 | 71 | 450 | 3 | 0 | 11 | 780 |
| Salsa | 1 | 62 | 320 | 3 | 0 | 3 | 800 |
| Wheat | 1 | 66 | 350 | 4 | 0 | 5 | 650 |
| **Muffins** | | | | | | | |
| Carrot Walnut Spice | 1 | 81 | 600 | 3 | 50 | 27 | 430 |
| Banana Walnut | 1 | 73 | 540 | 3 | 75 | 23 | 550 |

# DUNKIN' DONUTS – *continued*

## Muffins – *cont.*

| | Size | Carb (g) | Cal. (g) | Fiber (g) | Total Chol. (mg) | Fat (g) | Sod. (mg) |
|---|---|---|---|---|---|---|---|
| Blueberry | 1 | 75 | 490 | 2 | 75 | 18 | 630 |
| Blueberry, Reduced Fat | 1 | 74 | 450 | 2 | 70 | 13 | 650 |
| Chocolate Chip | 1 | 85 | 590 | 3 | 75 | 23 | 570 |
| Coffee Cake Muffin w/ Topping | 1 | 102 | 710 | 2 | 85 | 29 | 650 |
| Corn | 1 | 81 | 510 | 1 | 85 | 17 | 950 |
| Cranberry Orange | 1 | 71 | 460 | 3 | 70 | 16 | 530 |
| Honey Bran Raisin | 1 | 81 | 490 | 5 | 60 | 14 | 510 |
| **Danish** | | | | | | | |
| Apple | 1 | 36 | 250 | 0 | 5 | 10 | 220 |
| Cheese | 1 | 32 | 270 | 0 | 15 | 14 | 210 |
| Strawberry Cheese | 1 | 33 | 250 | 0 | 10 | 12 | 200 |
| **Donuts** | | | | | | | |
| Apple Crumb | 1 | 34 | 230 | 1 | 0 | 10 | 270 |
| Apple N' Spice | 1 | 29 | 200 | 1 | 0 | 8 | 270 |
| Bavarian Kreme | 1 | 30 | 210 | 1 | 0 | 9 | 270 |

# DUNKIN' DONUTS - *continued*

## Donuts - *cont.*

| | Size | Carb (g) | Cal. (g) | Fiber (g) | Total Chol. (mg) | Fat (g) | Sod. (mg) |
|---|---|---|---|---|---|---|---|
| Chocolate Iced Bismark | 1 | 50 | 340 | 1 | 0 | 15 | 290 |
| Black Raspberry | 1 | 32 | 210 | 1 | 0 | 8 | 280 |
| Blueberry Cake | 1 | 35 | 290 | 1 | 10 | 16 | 400 |
| Blueberry Crumb | 1 | 36 | 240 | 1 | 0 | 10 | 260 |
| Boston Kreme | 1 | 36 | 240 | 1 | 0 | 9 | 280 |
| Bow Tie | 1 | 34 | 300 | 1 | 0 | 17 | 340 |
| Chocolate Coconut Cake | 1 | 31 | 300 | 1 | 0 | 19 | 370 |
| Chocolate Frosted Cake | 1 | 40 | 360 | 1 | 25 | 20 | 350 |
| Chocolate Frosted | 1 | 29 | 200 | 1 | 0 | 9 | 260 |
| Chocolate Glazed Cake | 1 | 33 | 290 | 1 | 0 | 16 | 370 |
| Chocolate Kreme Filled | 1 | 35 | 270 | 1 | 0 | 13 | 260 |
| Cinnamon Cake | 1 | 34 | 330 | 1 | 25 | 20 | 340 |
| Double Chocolate Cake | 1 | 37 | 310 | 2 | 0 | 17 | 370 |
| Éclair | 1 | 39 | 270 | 1 | 0 | 11 | 290 |

# DUNKIN' DONUTS - *continued*

## Donuts - *cont.*

| | Size | Carb (g) | Cal. (g) | Fiber (g) | Total Chol. (mg) | Fat (g) | Sod. (mg) |
|---|---|---|---|---|---|---|---|
| Glazed Cake | 1 | 41 | 350 | 1 | 25 | 19 | 340 |
| French Cruller | 1 | 17 | 150 | 1 | 20 | 8 | 105 |
| **Miscellaneous Baked Goods** | | | | | | | |
| Apple Fritter | 1 | 41 | 300 | 1 | 0 | 14 | 360 |
| Biscuit | 1 | 29 | 250 | 1 | 0 | 13 | 780 |
| Coffee Roll | 1 | 33 | 270 | 1 | 0 | 14 | 340 |
| Chocolate Frosted Coffee Roll | 1 | 36 | 290 | 1 | 0 | 15 | 340 |
| Croissant, Plain | 1 | 37 | 330 | 0 | 5 | 18 | 270 |
| **Sandwiches** | | | | | | | |
| Biscuit/Egg/ Cheese | 1 | 31 | 360 | 1 | 125 | 20 | 1190 |
| Biscuit/ Sausage/Egg/ Cheese | 1 | 31 | 560 | 1 | 170 | 38 | 1700 |
| English Muffin/Ham/ Egg/Cheese | 1 | 35 | 310 | 1 | 145 | 10 | 1300 |
| **Cookies** | | | | | | | |
| Chocolate Chunk | 1 | 28 | 220 | 1 | 35 | 11 | 105 |

# DUNKIN' DONUTS – *continued*

## Cookies – *cont.*

| | Size | Carb (g) | Cal. (g) | Fiber (g) | Total Chol. (mg) | Fat (g) | Sod. (mg) |
|---|---|---|---|---|---|---|---|
| Chocolate Chunk w/ Nuts | 1 | 27 | 230 | 1 | 35 | 12 | 110 |
| Chocolate-White Chocolate Chunk | 1 | 28 | 230 | 1 | 35 | 12 | 120 |
| Oatmeal Raisin Pecan | 1 | 29 | 220 | 1 | 30 | 10 | 110 |
| **Beverages** | | | | | | | |
| Coffee Coolatta with 2% | 16 oz | 41 | 190 | 0 | 10 | 2 | 80 |
| Coffee Coolatta with Cream | 16 oz | 40 | 350 | 0 | 75 | 22 | 65 |
| Coolatta with Milk | 16 oz | 42 | 210 | 0 | 15 | 3 | 80 |
| Coolatta with Skim Milk | 16 oz | 41 | 170 | 0 | 0 | 0 | 80 |
| Iced Coffee with Skim Milk | 16 oz | 16 | 70 | 0 | 0 | 0 | 75 |
| Iced Coffee with Skim Milk and Sugar | 16 oz | 15 | 60 | 0 | 0 | 0 | 25 |
| Iced Coffee with Sugar | 16 oz | 15 | 60 | 0 | 0 | 0 | 70 |
| Orange Mango Fruit Coolatta | 16 oz | 69 | 280 | 1 | 0 | 0 | 35 |

# DUNKIN' DONUTS – *continued*

## Beverages – *cont.*

| | Size | Carb (g) | Cal. (g) | Fiber (g) | Total Chol. (mg) | Fat (g) | Sod. (mg) |
|---|---|---|---|---|---|---|---|
| Strawberry Fruit Coolatta | 16 oz | 68 | 270 | 1 | 0 | 0 | 35 |
| Vanilla Bean Coolatta | 16 oz | 73 | 440 | 0 | 0 | 17 | 100 |
| Vanilla Chai | 16 oz | 40 | 230 | 0 | 5 | 8 | 50 |

## KENTUCKY FRIED CHICKEN

| | Size | Carb (g) | Cal. (g) | Fiber (g) | Total Chol. (mg) | Fat (g) | Sod. (mg) |
|---|---|---|---|---|---|---|---|
| **Chicken** | | | | | | | |
| Extra Crunchy Breast | 1 | 19 | 460 | 0 | 135 | 28 | 1230 |
| Extra Crunchy Drumstick | 1 | 5 | 160 | 0 | 70 | 10 | 420 |
| Extra Crunchy Thigh | 1 | 12 | 370 | 0 | 120 | 26 | 710 |
| Extra Crunchy Whole Wing | 1 | 10 | 190 | 0 | 55 | 12 | 390 |
| Hot and Spicy Breast | 1 | 20 | 460 | 0 | 130 | 27 | 1450 |
| Hot and Spicy Drumstick | 1 | 4 | 150 | 0 | 65 | 9 | 380 |
| Hot and Spicy Thigh | 1 | 14 | 400 | 0 | 125 | 28 | 1240 |
| Hot and Spicy Whole Wing | 1 | 9 | 180 | 0 | 60 | 11 | 420 |
| Original Recipe Breast w/o skin | 1 | 0 | 140 | 0 | 95 | 3 | 410 |
| Original Recipe Drumstick | 1 | 4 | 140 | 0 | 75 | 8 | 440 |
| Original Recipe Thigh | 1 | 12 | 360 | 0 | 165 | 25 | 1060 |

## KENTUCKY FRIED CHICKEN - *continued*

### Chicken – *cont.*

| | Size | Carb (g) | Cal. (g) | Fiber (g) | Total Chol. (mg) | Fat (g) | Sod. (mg) |
|---|---|---|---|---|---|---|---|
| Original Recipe Breast | 1 | 11 | 380 | 0 | 145 | 19 | 1160 |
| Original Recipe Whole Wing | 1 | 5 | 150 | 0 | 60 | 9 | 370 |
| **Sandwiches** | | | | | | | |
| Original Recipe Sandwich | 1 | 22 | 450 | 0 | 65 | 27 | 1010 |
| Original Recipe Sand w/o sauce | 1 | 21 | 320 | 0 | 60 | 13 | 890 |
| Triple Crunch Sandwich with Sauce | 1 | 42 | 670 | 1 | 80 | 40 | 1640 |
| Triple Crunch Sandwich no sauce | 1 | 41 | 540 | 1 | 75 | 26 | 1510 |
| Tender Roast Sandwich | 1 | 24 | 390 | 1 | 70 | 19 | 810 |
| Tender Roast Sandwich w/o sauce | 1 | 23 | 260 | 1 | 65 | 5 | 690 |
| **Specialties** | | | | | | | |
| Chicken Pot Pie | 1 | 70 | 770 | 5 | 115 | 40 | 1680 |
| Crispy Strips | 1 | 17 | 400 | 0 | 75 | 24 | 1250 |

# KENTUCKY FRIED CHICKEN – *continued*

## Specialties – *cont.*

| | Size | Carb (g) | Cal. (g) | Fiber (g) | Total Chol. (mg) | Fat (g) | Sod. (mg) |
|---|---|---|---|---|---|---|---|
| Hot Wings | 6 | 23 | 450 | 1 | 145 | 29 | 1120 |
| Popcorn Chicken | Ind | 25 | 450 | 0 | 50 | 30 | 1030 |
| Popcorn Chicken | Lg | 37 | 660 | 0 | 75 | 44 | 1530 |
| **Sides** | | | | | | | |
| BBQ Beans | 1 | 46 | 230 | 7 | 0 | 1 | 720 |
| Biscuit | 1 | 23 | 190 | 0 | 1.5 | 10 | 580 |
| Cole Slaw | 1 | 22 | 190 | 3 | 5 | 11 | 300 |
| Corn on the Cob | Sm | 13 | 70 | 3 | 0 | 2 | 5 |
| Corn on the Cob | Lg | 26 | 150 | 7 | 0 | 3 | 10 |
| Green Beans | 1 | 5 | 50 | 2 | 5 | 2 | 460 |
| Mac and Cheese | 1 | 15 | 130 | 1 | 5 | 6 | 610 |
| Mashed Potatoes w/ Gravy | 1 | 18 | 120 | 1 | 0 | 5 | 380 |
| Mashed Potatoes w/o Gravy | 1 | 16 | 110 | 1 | 0 | 4 | 260 |
| Potato Salad | 1 | 22 | 180 | 1 | 5 | 9 | 470 |
| Potato Wedges | 1 | 30 | 240 | 3 | 0 | 12 | 830 |

## KENTUCKY FRIED CHICKEN - *continued*

| | Size | Carb (g) | Cal. (g) | Fiber (g) | Total Chol. (mg) | Fat (g) | Sod. (mg) |
|---|---|---|---|---|---|---|---|
| **Desserts** | | | | | | | |
| Apple Pie Slice | 1 | 45 | 270 | 4 | 0 | 9 | 200 |
| Cherry Cheesecake Parfait | 1 | 46 | 300 | 2 | 4 | 11 | 130 |

## LONG JOHN SILVER'S

| | Size | Carb (g) | Cal. (g) | Fiber (g) | Total Chol. (mg) | Fat (g) | Sod. (mg) |
|---|---|---|---|---|---|---|---|
| **Seafood** | | | | | | | |
| Battered Fish | 1 | 16 | 230 | 0 | 30 | 13 | 700 |
| Battered Shrimp | 1 | 3 | 45 | 0 | 15 | 3 | 125 |
| Battered Clams | 1 | 22 | 240 | 1 | 10 | 13 | 1110 |
| **Sandwiches** | | | | | | | |
| Fish Sandwich | 1 | 48 | 440 | 3 | 35 | 20 | 1120 |
| Ultimate Fish | 1 | 48 | 500 | 3 | 50 | 25 | 1310 |
| **Sides** | | | | | | | |
| Battered Chicken | 1 | 9 | 140 | 0 | 20 | 8 | 400 |
| Fries | Reg | 34 | 230 | 3 | 0 | 10 | 350 |
| Fries | Lg | 56 | 390 | 5 | 0 | 17 | 580 |
| Hushpuppies | 1 | 9 | 60 | 1 | 0 | 2.5 | 200 |
| Coleslaw | 1 | 15 | 200 | 3 | 20 | 15 | 340 |
| Rice | 1 | 34 | 180 | 3 | 0 | 4 | 540 |
| Corn Cobbet | 1 | 14 | 90 | 3 | 0 | 3 | 0 |

## LONG JOHN SILVER'S - *continued*

### Sides - *cont.*

| | Size | Carb (g) | Cal. (g) | Fiber (g) | Total Chol. (mg) | Fat (g) | Sod. (mg) |
|---|---|---|---|---|---|---|---|
| Cheese Sticks | 3 | 12 | 140 | 1 | 10 | 8 | 320 |

### Desserts

| | Size | Carb (g) | Cal. (g) | Fiber (g) | Total Chol. (mg) | Fat (g) | Sod. (mg) |
|---|---|---|---|---|---|---|---|
| Chocolate Cream Pie | 1 | 24 | 310 | 1 | 15 | 22 | 170 |
| Pecan Pie | 1 | 55 | 370 | 2 | 40 | 15 | 190 |

# MCDONALD'S

| | Size | Carb (g) | Cal. (g) | Fiber (g) | Total Chol. (mg) | Fat (g) | Sod. (mg) |
|---|---|---|---|---|---|---|---|
| **Burgers** | | | | | | | |
| Big Mac | 1 | 50 | 600 | 4 | 85 | 33 | 1050 |
| Big N' Tasty | 1 | 38 | 540 | 3 | 80 | 32 | 780 |
| Big N' Tasty w/ Cheese | 1 | 39 | 590 | 3 | 95 | 36 | 1020 |
| Hamburger | 1 | 36 | 280 | 2 | 30 | 10 | 550 |
| Cheeseburger | 1 | 36 | 330 | 2 | 45 | 14 | 790 |
| Double Cheeseburger | 1 | 38 | 490 | 2 | 85 | 26 | 1220 |
| Double Quarter Pounder w/ Chz | 1 | 39 | 770 | 3 | 165 | 47 | 1440 |
| Quarter Pounder | 1 | 38 | 430 | 3 | 70 | 21 | 770 |
| Quarter Pounder w/ Cheese | 1 | 39 | 540 | 3 | 95 | 29 | 1240 |
| **Sandwiches** | | | | | | | |
| Filet O' Fish | 1 | 41 | 410 | 1 | 45 | 20 | 660 |
| Chicken McGrill | 1 | 37 | 400 | 3 | 70 | 16 | 1020 |
| Crispy Chicken | 1 | 47 | 510 | 3 | 50 | 26 | 1090 |

## MCDONALD'S – *continued*

### Sandwiches - *cont.*

| | Size | Carb (g) | Cal. (g) | Fiber (g) | Total Chol. (mg) | Fat (g) | Sod. (mg) |
|---|---|---|---|---|---|---|---|
| Hot n' Spicy McChicken | 1 | 40 | 450 | 1 | 45 | 26 | 820 |
| McChicken | 1 | 41 | 430 | 3 | 45 | 23 | 830 |

### Salads

| | Size | Carb (g) | Cal. (g) | Fiber (g) | Total Chol. (mg) | Fat (g) | Sod. (mg) |
|---|---|---|---|---|---|---|---|
| Crispy Chicken Bacon Ranch Salad | 1 | 20 | 350 | 3 | 65 | 19 | 1000 |
| Crispy Chicken Caesar Salad | 1 | 20 | 310 | 3 | 50 | 16 | 890 |
| Crispy Chicken California Cobb Salad | 1 | 20 | 370 | 3 | 125 | 21 | 1130 |
| Grilled Chicken Bacon Ranch Salad | 1 | 9 | 250 | 3 | 85 | 10 | 930 |
| Grilled Chicken Caesar Salad | 1 | 9 | 200 | 3 | 70 | 6 | 820 |
| Grilled Chicken California Cobb Salad | 1 | 9 | 270 | 3 | 145 | 11 | 1060 |
| Side Salad | 1 | 3 | 15 | 1 | 0 | 0 | 10 |

## MCDONALD'S - *continued*

| | Size | Carb (g) | Cal. (g) | Fiber (g) | Total Chol. (mg) | Fat (g) | Sod. (mg) |
|---|---|---|---|---|---|---|---|
| **Salad Dressings** | | | | | | | |
| Newman's Own® Low Fat Balsamic Viniagrette | 1.5 oz | 4 | 40 | 0 | 0 | 3 | 730 |
| Newman's Own® Ranch | 2.0 oz | 9 | 170 | 0 | 20 | 15 | 530 |
| Newman's Own® Salsa | 3.0 oz | 7 | 30 | 1 | 0 | 0 | 290 |
| Newman's Own® Cobb | 2.0 oz | 9 | 120 | 0 | 10 | 9 | 440 |
| Newman's Own® Caesar | 2.0 oz | 4 | 190 | 0 | 20 | 18 | 500 |
| **Specialties and Sides** | | | | | | | |
| Chicken McNuggets | 6 | 15 | 250 | 0 | 35 | 15 | 670 |
| Chicken McNuggets | 10 | 26 | 420 | 0 | 60 | 24 | 1120 |
| French Fries | Sm | 26 | 210 | 2 | 0 | 10 | 135 |
| French Fries | Lg | 66 | 540 | 6 | 0 | 25 | 350 |
| **Breakfast** | | | | | | | |
| Bacon, Egg, & Cheese McGriddle | 1 | 43 | 440 | 1 | 240 | 21 | 1270 |

## MCDONALD'S – *continued*

### Breakfast – *cont.*

| | Size | Carb (g) | Cal. (g) | Fiber (g) | Total Chol. (mg) | Fat (g) | Sod. (mg) |
|---|---|---|---|---|---|---|---|
| Sausage, Egg & Cheese McGriddle | 1 | 43 | 550 | 1 | 260 | 33 | 1290 |
| Sausage McGriddle | 1 | 42 | 420 | 1 | 35 | 23 | 970 |
| Egg McMuffin | 1 | 28 | 300 | 2 | 235 | 12 | 840 |
| Sausage McMuffin | 1 | 28 | 370 | 2 | 50 | 23 | 790 |
| Sausage McMuffin w/Egg | 1 | 29 | 450 | 2 | 260 | 28 | 930 |
| English Muffin | 1 | 27 | 150 | 2 | 0 | 2 | 270 |
| Bacon, Egg & Cheese Biscuit | 1 | 31 | 460 | 1 | 245 | 28 | 1370 |
| Sausage Biscuit | 1 | 30 | 410 | 1 | 35 | 28 | 930 |
| Sausage Biscuit w/ Egg | 1 | 31 | 490 | 1 | 245 | 33 | 1010 |
| Biscuit | 1 | 30 | 240 | 1 | 0 | 11 | 640 |
| Ham, Egg, & Cheese Bagel | 1 | 58 | 550 | 2 | 255 | 23 | 1500 |

# PIZZA HUT

| | Size | Carb (g) | Cal. (g) | Fiber (g) | Total Chol. (mg) | Fat (g) | Sod. (mg) |
|---|---|---|---|---|---|---|---|
| **Pizza** | | | | | | | |
| **Stuffed Crust Pizza- 14" Slice** | | | | | | | |
| Cheese | 1 | 43 | 360 | 2 | 40 | 13 | 920 |
| Ham | 1 | 42 | 340 | 3 | 40 | 12 | 960 |
| Pepperoni | 1 | 42 | 370 | 3 | 45 | 15 | 970 |
| Meat Lover's | 1 | 43 | 450 | 3 | 55 | 21 | 1250 |
| Veggie Lover's | 1 | 45 | 360 | 3 | 35 | 14 | 980 |
| Supreme | 1 | 44 | 400 | 3 | 45 | 16 | 1070 |
| Super Supreme | 1 | 45 | 440 | 3 | 50 | 20 | 1270 |
| **Thin n' Crispy Pizza- 14" Slice** | | | | | | | |
| Cheese | 1 | 20 | 190 | 1 | 25 | 8 | 460 |
| Ham | 1 | 19 | 170 | 1 | 20 | 6 | 520 |
| Pepperoni | 1 | 19 | 200 | 1 | 25 | 10 | 520 |
| Sausage Lover's | 1 | 20 | 230 | 1 | 30 | 12 | 590 |
| Meat Lover's | 1 | 20 | 250 | 2 | 35 | 14 | 700 |
| Veggie Lover's | 1 | 21 | 170 | 2 | 15 | 7 | 480 |

# PIZZA HUT – *continued*

## Thin n' Crispy Pizza – *cont.*

|  | Size | Carb (g) | Cal. (g) | Fiber (g) | Total Chol. (mg) | Fat (g) | Sod. (mg) |
|---|---|---|---|---|---|---|---|
| Pepperoni Lover's | 1 | 20 | 260 | 2 | 35 | 14 | 660 |
| Supreme | 1 | 21 | 220 | 2 | 25 | 11 | 640 |
| Super Supreme | 1 | 21 | 260 | 2 | 35 | 13 | 760 |
| **P'Zone** | | | | | | | |
| Pepperoni | 1/2 | 69 | 610 | 3 | 55 | 22 | 1280 |
| Meat Lover's | 1/2 | 70 | 680 | 3 | 65 | 28 | 1540 |
| **Appetizers** | | | | | | | |
| Mild Buffalo Wings | 2 | 0 | 110 | 0 | 70 | 7 | 320 |
| Hot Buffalo Wings | 2 | 1 | 110 | 0 | 70 | 6 | 450 |

# SONIC

| | Size | Carb (g) | Cal. (g) | Fiber (g) | Total Chol. (mg) | Fat (g) | Sod. (mg) |
|---|---|---|---|---|---|---|---|
| **Burgers** | | | | | | | |
| No.1 Sonic Burger | 1 | 43 | 577 | 2 | 37 | 36 | 753 |
| No. 2 Sonic Burger | 1 | 43 | 481 | 2 | 29 | 25 | 761 |
| No. 1 Sonic Cheeseburger | 1 | 44 | 647 | 2 | 52 | 42 | 1103 |
| No. 2 Sonic Cheeseburger | 1 | 44 | 551 | 2 | 44 | 31 | 1111 |
| Bacon Cheeseburger | 1 | 44 | 727 | 2 | 67 | 49 | 1433 |
| SuperSonic No. 1 | 1 | 45 | 929 | 2 | 96 | 66 | 1476 |
| SuperSonic No. 2 | 1 | 46 | 839 | 3 | 88 | 55 | 1571 |
| Jr. Burger | 1 | 27 | 353 | 1 | 45 | 21 | 1294 |
| **Toaster Sandwiches** | | | | | | | |
| Grilled Cheese | 1 | 39 | 282 | 2 | 15 | 12 | 830 |
| BLT | 1 | 42 | 581 | 3 | 47 | 41 | 1307 |
| Bacon Cheddar Burger | 1 | 60 | 675 | 4 | 59 | 38 | 1786 |
| Chicken Club | 1 | 75 | 675 | 3 | 85 | 29 | 1458 |

**SONIC** - *continued*

## Toaster Sandwiches - *cont.*

| | Size | Carb (g) | Cal. (g) | Fiber (g) | Total Chol. (mg) | Fat (g) | Sod. (mg) |
|---|---|---|---|---|---|---|---|
| Country Fried Steak | 1 | 55 | 708 | 3 | 60 | 45 | 944 |
| Country Fried Steak Sandwich | 1 | 56 | 748 | 2 | 60 | 47 | 804 |

## Chicken

| | Size | Carb (g) | Cal. (g) | Fiber (g) | Total Chol. (mg) | Fat (g) | Sod. (mg) |
|---|---|---|---|---|---|---|---|
| Chicken Strip Dinner | 1 | 86 | 749 | 5 | 47 | 32 | 1973 |
| Chicken Strip Snack | 1 | 22 | 272 | 0 | 35 | 13 | 760 |
| Grilled Chicken Sandwich | 1 | 31 | 343 | 2 | 70 | 13 | 829 |
| Breaded Chicken Sandwich | 1 | 66 | 582 | 2 | 53 | 23 | 427 |

## Coneys

| | Size | Carb (g) | Cal. (g) | Fiber (g) | Total Chol. (mg) | Fat (g) | Sod. (mg) |
|---|---|---|---|---|---|---|---|
| Regular Cheese Coney | 1 | 24 | 366 | 1 | 52 | 24 | 962 |
| Regular Coney Plain | 1 | 22 | 262 | 1 | 30 | 16 | 657 |
| Extra Long Cheese Coney | 1 | 47 | 666 | 2 | 87 | 42 | 1648 |
| Extra Long Coney Plain | 1 | 44 | 483 | 1 | 50 | 27 | 1162 |
| Corn Dog | 1 | 23 | 262 | 1 | 15 | 17 | 480 |

## SONIC – *continued*

| | Size | Carb (g) | Cal. (g) | Fiber (g) | Total Chol. (mg) | Fat (g) | Sod. (mg) |
|---|---|---|---|---|---|---|---|
| **Wraps** | | | | | | | |
| Grilled Chicken Wrap | 1 | 40 | 539 | 2 | 70 | 27 | 1035 |
| Grilled Chicken wrap w/o Ranch | 1 | 38 | 393 | 2 | 65 | 12 | 820 |
| Chicken Strip Wrap | 1 | 55 | 574 | 2 | 28 | 29 | 1071 |
| Chicken Strip Wrap w/o Ranch | 1 | 53 | 428 | 2 | 23 | 13 | 856 |
| Fritos Chili Cheese Wrap | 1 | 68 | 743 | 5 | 52 | 42 | 1172 |
| **Sides** | | | | | | | |
| French Fries | Reg | 22 | 195 | 4 | 0 | 11 | 648 |
| French Fries | Lg | 30 | 252 | 5 | 0 | 13 | 758 |
| Cheese Fries | Reg | 23 | 265 | 4 | 15 | 17 | 998 |
| Cheese Fries | Lg | 31 | 322 | 5 | 15 | 19 | 1108 |
| Chili Cheese Fries | Reg | 24 | 299 | 4 | 22 | 19 | 952 |
| Chili Cheese Fries | Lg | 32 | 357 | 5 | 22 | 22 | 1062 |
| Super Sonic Fries | SS | 44 | 358 | 7 | 0 | 18 | 963 |
| Tater Tots | Reg | 27 | 259 | 3 | 0 | 16 | 1046 |

**SONIC** – *continued*

**Sides** – *cont.*

| | Size | Carb (g) | Cal. (g) | Fiber (g) | Total Chol. (mg) | Fat (g) | Sod. (mg) |
|---|---|---|---|---|---|---|---|
| Tater Tots | Lg | 40 | 365 | 4 | 0 | 21 | 1358 |
| Cheese Tater Tots | Reg | 28 | 329 | 3 | 15 | 22 | 1396 |
| Cheese Tater Tots | Lg | 41 | 435 | 4 | 15 | 27 | 1708 |
| Chili Cheese Tater Tots | Reg | 28 | 363 | 3 | 22 | 25 | 1350 |
| Chili Cheese Tater Tots | Lg | 43 | 547 | 5 | 37 | 36 | 1844 |
| Super Sonic Tots | SS | 53 | 485 | 5 | 0 | 28 | 1670 |
| Onion Rings | Reg | 66 | 331 | 7 | 0 | 5 | 311 |
| Onion Rings | Lg | 102 | 507 | 10 | 0 | 7 | 486 |
| Sonic Onion Rings | SS | 141 | 706 | 11 | 1 | 10 | 788 |
| Fritos Chili Pie | 1 | 36 | 611 | 3 | 53 | 44 | 816 |
| Mozzarella Sticks | 1 | 35 | 382 | 0 | 50 | 19 | 1300 |
| Ched R' Peppers | 1 | 29 | 256 | 4 | 28 | 12 | 1056 |

**Breakfast**

| | Size | Carb (g) | Cal. (g) | Fiber (g) | Total Chol. (mg) | Fat (g) | Sod. (mg) |
|---|---|---|---|---|---|---|---|
| Bacon, Egg and Cheese Toaster | 1 | 40 | 500 | 2 | 156 | 29 | 1698 |

**SONIC** – *continued*

**Breakfast** – *cont.*

| | Size | Carb (g) | Cal. (g) | Fiber (g) | Total Chol. (mg) | Fat (g) | Sod. (mg) |
|---|---|---|---|---|---|---|---|
| Sausage, Egg and Cheese Toaster | 1 | 44 | 570 | 2 | 126 | 36 | 1038 |
| Ham, Egg and Cheese Toaster | 1 | 41 | 436 | 2 | 174 | 19 | 2079 |
| Breakfast Burrito | 1 | 45 | 616 | 3 | 167 | 37 | 1535 |
| Sonic Sunrise | Reg | 60 | 224 | 1 | 0 | 0 | 41 |
| Sonic Sunrise | Lg | 100 | 368 | 2 | 0 | 0 | 72 |

# SUBWAY

| | Size | Carb (g) | Cal. (g) | Fiber (g) | Total Chol. (mg) | Fat (g) | Sod. (mg) |
|---|---|---|---|---|---|---|---|
| **6" Sandwiches** | | | | | | | |
| Tuna | 6" | 46 | 430 | 4 | 45 | 19 | 1070 |
| Veggie Delite | 6" | 44 | 230 | 4 | 0 | 3 | 510 |
| Subway Seafood Sensation | 6" | 52 | 380 | 5 | 25 | 13 | 1170 |
| Italian BMT | 6" | 47 | 450 | 4 | 55 | 21 | 1790 |
| Cold Cut Combo | 6" | 46 | 410 | 4 | 55 | 17 | 1570 |
| Cheese Steak | 6" | 47 | 360 | 5 | 35 | 10 | 1090 |
| Meatball Marinara | 6" | 53 | 500 | 5 | 45 | 11 | 1290 |
| **Select Sandwiches** | | | | | | | |
| Sweet Onion Chicken Teriyaki | 6" | 59 | 370 | 4 | 50 | 5 | 1090 |
| Honey Mustard Ham | 6" | 54 | 310 | 4 | 25 | 5 | 1410 |
| Chipotle Southwest Steak and Cheese | 6" | 49 | 440 | 5 | 45 | 19 | 1160 |
| **Atkins-Friendly Wraps** | | | | | | | |
| Chicken Bacon Ranch - **8 net carbs** | 6" | 19 | 480 | 11 | 90 | 26 | 1340 |

# SUBWAY – *continued*

## Atkins Friendly Wraps – *cont.*

| | Size | Carb (g) | Cal. (g) | Fiber (g) | Total Chol. (mg) | Fat (g) | Sod. (mg) |
|---|---|---|---|---|---|---|---|
| Turkey Bacon Melt - **10 net carbs** | 6" | 22 | 430 | 12 | 65 | 25 | 1650 |
| Turkey Breast and Ham - **10 net carbs** | 6" | 19 | 390 | 9 | 60 | 23 | 1890 |

## Double Meat Extreme Subs

| | Size | Carb (g) | Cal. (g) | Fiber (g) | Total Chol. (mg) | Fat (g) | Sod. (mg) |
|---|---|---|---|---|---|---|---|
| Turkey Breast | 6" | 48 | 330 | 4 | 40 | 5 | 1510 |
| Turkey Breast and Ham | 6" | 48 | 360 | 4 | 45 | 7 | 1930 |
| Ham | 6" | 49 | 350 | 4 | 50 | 7 | 2030 |
| Roast Beef | 6" | 46 | 360 | 4 | 40 | 7 | 1310 |
| Chicken | 6" | 50 | 430 | 5 | 90 | 8 | 1510 |
| Tuna | 6" | 48 | 580 | 4 | 75 | 32 | 1430 |
| Seafood Sensation | 6" | 60 | 490 | 5 | 35 | 20 | 1620 |
| Italian BMT | 6" | 49 | 630 | 4 | 100 | 35 | 2860 |
| Cold Cut Combo | 6" | 48 | 550 | 4 | 105 | 28 | 2420 |
| Meatball | 6" | 61 | 740 | 5 | 85 | 38 | 1640 |
| Sweet Onion Chicken Teriyaki | 6" | 59 | 450 | 4 | 100 | 7 | 1400 |
| Chipotle Southwest Steak and Cheese | 6" | 52 | 530 | 6 | 70 | 22 | 1530 |

## SUBWAY – *continued*

| | Size | Carb (g) | Cal. (g) | Fiber (g) | Total Chol. (mg) | Fat (g) | Sod. (mg) |
|---|---|---|---|---|---|---|---|
| **Soup** | | | | | | | |
| Roasted Chicken Noodle | 1 | 7 | 60 | 1 | 10 | 1.5 | 940 |
| Vegetable Beef | 1 | 15 | 90 | 3 | 5 | 1 | 1050 |
| Cream of Potato with Bacon | 1 | 21 | 200 | 2 | 15 | 11 | 840 |
| Cheese with Ham & Bacon | 1 | 17 | 240 | 1 | 20 | 15 | 1160 |
| Cream of Broccoli | 1 | 15 | 130 | 2 | 10 | 6 | 860 |
| Minestrone | 1 | 7 | 90 | 2 | 20 | 4 | 1180 |
| New England Clam Chowder | 1 | 16 | 110 | 1 | 10 | 3.5 | 990 |
| Chicken and Dumplings | 1 | 16 | 130 | 1 | 30 | 5 | 1030 |
| Brown and Wild Rice with Chicken | 1 | 17 | 190 | 2 | 20 | 11 | 990 |
| Chili Con Carne | 1 | 23 | 240 | 8 | 15 | 10 | 860 |

## SUBWAY – *continued*

| | Size | Carb (g) | Cal. (g) | Fiber (g) | Total Chol. (mg) | Fat (g) | Sod. (mg) |
|---|---|---|---|---|---|---|---|
| **Salads** | | | | | | | |
| Classic Club w/o dressing **9 net carbs** | 1 | 13 | 390 | 4 | 210 | 21 | 1820 |
| Garden Fresh w/o dressing | 1 | 11 | 60 | 5 | 0 | 1 | 80 |
| Grilled Chicken and Spinach w/o dressing **5 net carbs** | 1 | 10 | 420 | 5 | 215 | 26 | 970 |
| Mediterranean Chicken w/o dressing | 1 | 11 | 170 | 5 | 55 | 4.5 | 520 |
| **Dressings** | | | | | | | |
| Greek Vinaigrette | 1 | 3 | 200 | 0 | 0 | 21 | 590 |
| Red Wine Vinaigrette | 1 | 17 | 80 | 0 | 0 | 1 | 910 |
| Atkins Honey-Mustard **1 net carb** | 1 | 1 | 200 | 0 | 0 | 22 | 510 |
| Kraft Fat-free Italian | 1 | 7 | 35 | 0 | 0 | 0 | 720 |
| Kraft Ranch - **.5 net carbs** | 1 | 1 | 200 | 1 | 10 | 22 | 550 |

## SUBWAY – *continued*

| | Size | Carb (g) | Cal. (g) | Fiber (g) | Total Chol. (mg) | Fat (g) | Sod. (mg) |
|---|---|---|---|---|---|---|---|
| **Cookies and Desserts** | | | | | | | |
| Chocolate Chip Cookie | 1 | 30 | 210 | 1 | 15 | 10 | 160 |
| Oatmeal Raisin Cookie | 1 | 30 | 200 | 2 | 15 | 8 | 170 |
| Peanut Butter Cookie | 1 | 26 | 220 | 1 | 10 | 12 | 200 |
| M & M Cookie | 1 | 30 | 210 | 1 | 15 | 10 | 105 |
| White Macadamia Nut Cookie | 1 | 28 | 220 | 1 | 15 | 11 | 160 |
| Sugar Cookie | 1 | 28 | 230 | 0 | 15 | 12 | 135 |
| Chocolate Chunk Cookie | 1 | 30 | 220 | 1 | 10 | 10 | 105 |
| Double Chocolate Chip Cookie | 1 | 30 | 210 | 1 | 15 | 10 | 170 |
| Apple Pie | 1 | 37 | 245 | 1 | 0 | 10 | 290 |
| Fruit Roll Up | 1 | 12 | 50 | 0 | 0 | 1 | 55 |
| Atkins-Friendly Double Chocolate | 1 | 17 | 100 | 5 | 10 | 6 | 135 |

**SUBWAY** – *continued*

| | Size | Carb (g) | Cal. (g) | Fiber (g) | Total Chol. (mg) | Fat (g) | Sod. (mg) |
|---|---|---|---|---|---|---|---|
| **Breakfast Sandwiches on Deli Round** | | | | | | | |
| Cheese and Egg | 1 | 34 | 320 | 3 | 185 | 15 | 550 |
| Bacon and Egg | 1 | 34 | 320 | 3 | 185 | 15 | 520 |
| Western and Egg | 1 | 36 | 300 | 3 | 180 | 12 | 530 |
| Steak and Egg | 1 | 35 | 330 | 3 | 190 | 14 | 570 |
| Ham and Egg | 1 | 34 | 310 | 3 | 190 | 13 | 720 |
| Vegetable and Egg | 1 | 36 | 290 | 3 | 175 | 12 | 430 |
| **Breakfast Sandwiches on Italian or Wheat** | | | | | | | |
| Cheese and Egg | 6" | 42 | 440 | 3 | 570 | 19 | 730 |
| Bacon and Egg | 6" | 42 | 450 | 3 | 570 | 19 | 700 |
| Western and Egg | 6" | 44 | 430 | 4 | 565 | 17 | 710 |
| Steak and Egg | 6" | 43 | 460 | 4 | 575 | 18 | 750 |
| Ham and Egg | 6" | 42 | 430 | 3 | 575 | 17 | 900 |
| Vegetable and Egg | 6" | 44 | 410 | 4 | 560 | 16 | 610 |

**SUBWAY** – *continued*

| | Size | Carb (g) | Cal. (g) | Fiber (g) | Total Chol. (mg) | Fat (g) | Sod. (mg) |
|---|---|---|---|---|---|---|---|
| **Omelets & French Toast** | | | | | | | |
| Cheese and Egg | 1 | 2 | 240 | 0 | 570 | 17 | 370 |
| Bacon and Egg | 1 | 2 | 240 | 0 | 570 | 17 | 350 |
| Western and Egg | 1 | 4 | 220 | 1 | 565 | 14 | 360 |
| Steak and Egg | 1 | 3 | 250 | 1 | 580 | 15 | 390 |
| Ham and Egg | 1 | 2 | 230 | 0 | 575 | 14 | 550 |
| Vegetable and Egg | 1 | 4 | 210 | 1 | 560 | 14 | 250 |
| French Toast | 1 | 57 | 350 | 2 | 280 | 8 | 350 |

# TACO BELL

|  | Size | Carb (g) | Cal. (g) | Fiber (g) | Total Chol. (mg) | Fat (g) | Sod. (mg) |
|---|---|---|---|---|---|---|---|
| **Burritos** | | | | | | | |
| Bean Burrito | 1 | 55 | 370 | 8 | 10 | 10 | 1200 |
| Burrito Supreme-Chicken | 1 | 50 | 410 | 5 | 45 | 14 | 1270 |
| Chili Cheese Burrito | 1 | 40 | 390 | 3 | 40 | 18 | 1080 |
| Fiesta Burrito- Beef | 1 | 50 | 390 | 5 | 25 | 15 | 1150 |
| Fiesta Burrito-Chicken | 1 | 48 | 370 | 3 | 30 | 12 | 1090 |
| 7 Layer Burrito | 1 | 67 | 530 | 10 | 25 | 22 | 1360 |
| Burrito Supreme Beef | 1 | 51 | 440 | 7 | 40 | 18 | 1330 |
| Grilled Stuft Burrito-Beef | 1 | 79 | 730 | 10 | 65 | 33 | 2080 |
| Grilled Stuft Burrito-Chicken | 1 | 76 | 680 | 7 | 70 | 26 | 1950 |
| **Chalupas** | | | | | | | |
| Baja Chalupa-Chicken | 1 | 30 | 400 | 2 | 40 | 24 | 690 |

# TACO BELL – *continued*

## Chalupas – *cont.*

| | Size | Carb (g) | Cal. (g) | Fiber (g) | Total Chol. (mg) | Fat (g) | Sod. (mg) |
|---|---|---|---|---|---|---|---|
| Chalupa Supreme- Beef | 1 | 31 | 390 | 3 | 40 | 24 | 600 |
| Chalupa Supreme- Chicken | 1 | 30 | 370 | 1 | 45 | 20 | 530 |
| Nacho Chz Chalupa- Beef | 1 | 33 | 380 | 3 | 20 | 22 | 740 |
| Nacho Chz Chalupa- Chicken | 1 | 31 | 350 | 1 | 25 | 18 | 670 |
| **Enchiritos** | | | | | | | |
| Enchirito- Beef | 1 | 35 | 380 | 6 | 45 | 18 | 1430 |
| Enchirito- Steak | 1 | 34 | 360 | 5 | 45 | 16 | 1350 |
| Enchirito- Chicken | 1 | 34 | 350 | 5 | 55 | 14 | 1360 |
| **Gorditas** | | | | | | | |
| Baja Gordita- Beef | 1 | 31 | 350 | 4 | 30 | 19 | 750 |
| Baja Gordita- Chicken | 1 | 29 | 320 | 2 | 40 | 15 | 690 |
| Gordita Supreme- Beef | 1 | 30 | 310 | 3 | 35 | 16 | 590 |
| Gordita Supreme- Chicken | 1 | 28 | 290 | 2 | 45 | 12 | 530 |

# TACO BELL – *continued*

## Gorditas – *cont.*

| | Size | Carb (g) | Cal. (g) | Fiber (g) | Total Chol. (mg) | Fat (g) | Sod. (mg) |
|---|---|---|---|---|---|---|---|
| Nacho Chz Gordita-Beef | 1 | 32 | 300 | 3 | 20 | 13 | 740 |
| Nacho Chz Gordita-Chicken | 1 | 30 | 270 | 2 | 25 | 10 | 670 |
| **Nachos** | | | | | | | |
| Nacho Bellgrande | 1 | 80 | 780 | 12 | 35 | 43 | 1300 |
| Nacho Supreme | 1 | 42 | 450 | 7 | 35 | 26 | 800 |
| Nachos | 1 | 33 | 320 | 2 | <5 | 19 | 530 |
| **Salads** | | | | | | | |
| Taco Salad- w/o Shell | 1 | 33 | 420 | 11 | 65 | 21 | 1400 |
| Taco Salad w/ Salsa | 1 | 73 | 790 | 13 | 65 | 42 | 1670 |
| Express Taco Salad- With Chips | 1 | 60 | 620 | 13 | 65 | 31 | 1390 |
| **Sides** | | | | | | | |
| Guacamole | 1 | 2 | 35 | 1 | n/a | 3 | 100 |
| Mexican Rice | 1 | 23 | 210 | 3 | 15 | 10 | 740 |
| Pintos and Cheese | 1 | 20 | 180 | 6 | 15 | 7 | 700 |

# TACO BELL – *continued*

## Sides – *cont.*

| | Size | Carb (g) | Cal. (g) | Fiber (g) | Total Chol. (mg) | Fat (g) | Sod. (mg) |
|---|---|---|---|---|---|---|---|
| Cinnamon Twists | 1 | 28 | 160 | 0 | 0 | 5 | 150 |

## Specialties

| | Size | Carb (g) | Cal. (g) | Fiber (g) | Total Chol. (mg) | Fat (g) | Sod. (mg) |
|---|---|---|---|---|---|---|---|
| Taco | 1 | 13 | 170 | 3 | 25 | 10 | 350 |
| Taco Supreme | 1 | 14 | 220 | 3 | 40 | 14 | 360 |
| Soft Taco Chicken | 1 | 19 | 190 | <1 | 30 | 6 | 550 |
| Soft Taco Supreme- Chicken | 1 | 21 | 230 | 1 | 45 | 10 | 570 |
| Soft Taco Beef | 1 | 21 | 210 | 2 | 25 | 10 | 620 |
| Soft Taco Supreme- Beef | 1 | 22 | 260 | 3 | 40 | 14 | 630 |
| Grilled Steak Soft Taco | 1 | 21 | 280 | 1 | 30 | 17 | 650 |
| Double Decker Taco | 1 | 39 | 340 | 6 | 30 | 14 | 800 |
| Double Decker Taco Supreme | 1 | 40 | 380 | 7 | 40 | 18 | 820 |
| Cheese Quesadilla | 1 | 39 | 490 | 3 | 55 | 28 | 1150 |
| Chicken Quesadilla | 1 | 40 | 540 | 3 | 80 | 30 | 1380 |
| Fresco Mexican Pizza | 1 | 47 | 450 | 7 | - | 23 | 850 |
| Mexi Melt | 1 | 23 | 290 | 3 | 45 | 16 | 880 |

**TACO BELL** – *continued*

**Specialties** – *cont.*

| | Size | Carb (g) | Cal. (g) | Fiber (g) | Total Chol. (mg) | Fat (g) | Sod. (mg) |
|---|---|---|---|---|---|---|---|
| Mexican Pizza | 1 | 46 | 550 | 7 | 45 | 31 | 1030 |
| Southwest Steak Bowl | 1 | 73 | 700 | 13 | 55 | 32 | 2050 |
| Tostada | 1 | 29 | 250 | 7 | 15 | 10 | 710 |
| Zesty Chicken Bowl | 1 | 65 | 730 | 12 | 45 | 42 | 1640 |

# WENDY'S

| | Size | Carb (g) | Cal. (g) | Fiber (g) | Total Chol. (mg) | Fat (g) | Sod. (mg) |
|---|---|---|---|---|---|---|---|
| **Burgers** | | | | | | | |
| Jr. Hamburger | 1 | 34 | 270 | 2 | 30 | 9 | 610 |
| Jr. Cheeseburger | 1 | 34 | 310 | 2 | 45 | 12 | 820 |
| Jr. Cheeseburger Deluxe™ | 1 | 36 | 350 | 2 | 45 | 15 | 880 |
| Jr. Bacon Cheeseburger | 1 | 34 | 380 | 2 | 55 | 19 | 830 |
| Classic Single® w/ Everything | 1 | 37 | 410 | 2 | 70 | 19 | 910 |
| Big Bacon Classic® | 1 | 45 | 580 | 3 | 95 | 29 | 1430 |
| **Sandwiches** | | | | | | | |
| Ultimate Grilled Chicken Sandwich | 1 | 44 | 360 | 2 | 75 | 7 | 1100 |
| Spicy Chicken Sandwich | 1 | 57 | 510 | 2 | 55 | 19 | 1480 |
| **Salads** | | | | | | | |
| Mandarin Chicken Salad | 1 | 50 | 630 | 5 | 50 | 35 | 1540 |
| Mandarin Ckn Salad- salad only | 1 | 17 | 190 | 3 | 50 | 25 | 740 |

## WENDY'S – *continued*

| | Size | Carb (g) | Cal. (g) | Fiber (g) | Total Chol. (mg) | Fat (g) | Sod. (mg) |
|---|---|---|---|---|---|---|---|
| Spring Mix Salad | 1 | 25 | 500 | 7 | 30 | 42 | 1045 |
| Spring Mix Salad-Salad only | 1 | 12 | 180 | 5 | 30 | 11 | 230 |
| Chicken BLT Salad-Salad only | 1 | 10 | 360 | 4 | 95 | 19 | 1140 |
| Taco Supremo Salad | 1 | 64 | 670 | 10 | 85 | 32 | 1750 |
| Taco Supremo Salad- Salad only | 1 | 29 | 360 | 8 | 65 | 16 | 1090 |
| Caesar Side Salad | 1 | 12 | 290 | 1 | 30 | 23 | 550 |
| Caesar Side Salad-Salad only | 1 | 2 | 70 | 1 | 10 | 5 | 190 |
| Side Salad | 1 | 7 | 35 | 3 | 0 | 0 | 20 |
| **Dressings** | | | | | | | |
| Creamy Ranch | 1 Pkt | 5 | 230 | 0 | 15 | 23 | 580 |
| Fat Free French | 1 Pkt | 19 | 80 | 0 | 0 | 0 | 210 |
| Reduced Fat Creamy Ranch | 1 Pkt | 6 | 100 | 1 | 15 | 8 | 550 |
| Low Fat Honey Mustard | 1 Pkt | 21 | 110 | 0 | 0 | 3 | 340 |

# WENDY'S - *continued*

| | Size | Carb (g) | Cal. (g) | Fiber (g) | Total Chol. (mg) | Fat (g) | Sod. (mg) |
|---|---|---|---|---|---|---|---|
| **Specialties** | | | | | | | |
| Chicken Nuggets | 5 | 13 | 220 | 0 | 35 | 14 | 490 |
| Chicken Strips | 3 | 33 | 410 | 0 | 60 | 18 | 1470 |
| Chili | Sm | 21 | 200 | 5 | 35 | 5 | 870 |
| Chili | Lg | 31 | 300 | 7 | 50 | 7 | 1310 |
| Chili w/ Chz | Sm | 22 | 270 | 7 | 50 | 13 | 980 |
| **Sides & Dipping Sauces** | | | | | | | |
| Baked Potato | 1 | 61 | 270 | 7 | 0 | 0 | 25 |
| Baked Potato w/ Bacon and Chz | 1 | 67 | 560 | 7 | 35 | 23 | 910 |
| Baked Potato w/ Broc and Chz | 1 | 70 | 440 | 9 | 10 | 15 | 540 |
| Baked Potato w/ margarine | 1 | 67 | 330 | 7 | 0 | 7 | 140 |
| French Fries | Md | 56 | 390 | 6 | 0 | 17 | 340 |
| French Fries-Biggie | Bg | 63 | 440 | 7 | 0 | 19 | 380 |
| Deli Honey Mustard | 1 Pkt | 6 | 170 | 0 | 15 | 16 | 190 |

# WENDY'S – *continued*

## Sides & Dipping Sauces – *cont.*

|  | Size | Carb (g) | Cal. (g) | Fiber (g) | Total Chol. (mg) | Fat (g) | Sod. (mg) |
|---|---|---|---|---|---|---|---|
| Spicy Southwest Chipotle Sauce | 1 Pkt | 5 | 170 | 0 | 10 | 17 | 150 |
| Heartland Ranch | 1 Pkt | 1 | 200 | 0 | 20 | 21 | 280 |

## Desserts

|  | Size | Carb (g) | Cal. (g) | Fiber (g) | Total Chol. (mg) | Fat (g) | Sod. (mg) |
|---|---|---|---|---|---|---|---|
| Frosty | Jr. | 28 | 160 | 0 | 15 | 4 | 75 |
| Frosty | Md | 74 | 430 | 0 | 45 | 11 | 200 |

# DRINKS

## (Sizes Vary by Restaurant)

|  | Size | Carb (g) | Cal. (g) | Fiber (g) | Total Chol. (mg) | Fat (g) | Sod. (mg) |
|---|---|---|---|---|---|---|---|
| Coffee | Sm | 0 | 0 | 0 | 0 | 0 | 0 |
| Coffee | Md | 0 | 5 | 0 | 0 | 0 | 5 |
| Coffee | Lg | 0 | 10 | 0 | 0 | 0 | 10 |
| Coke | Sm | 40 | 150 | 0 | 0 | 0 | 15 |
| Coke | Md | 58 | 210 | 0 | 0 | 0 | 20 |
| Coke | Lg | 86 | 310 | 0 | 0 | 0 | 30 |
| Diet Coke | Sm | 0 | 0 | 0 | 0 | 0 | 30 |
| Diet Coke | Md | 0 | 0 | 0 | 0 | 0 | 40 |
| Diet Coke | Lg | 0 | 0 | 0 | 0 | 0 | 60 |
| Diet Pepsi | Sm | 0 | 0 | 0 | 0 | 0 | 35 |
| Diet Pepsi | Md | 0 | 0 | 0 | 0 | 0 | 45 |
| Diet Pepsi | Lg | 0 | 0 | 0 | 0 | 0 | 70 |
| Dr. Pepper | Sm | 39 | 144 | 0 | 0 | 0 | 50 |
| Dr. Pepper | Md | 47 | 175 | 0 | 0 | 0 | 61 |
| Dr. Pepper | Lg | 81 | 300 | 0 | 0 | 0 | 105 |

**DRINKS** – *cont.*

| | Size | Carb (g) | Cal. (g) | Fiber (g) | Total Chol. (mg) | Fat (g) | Sod. (mg) |
|---|---|---|---|---|---|---|---|
| Frozen Coke | Sm | 92 | 370 | 0 | 0 | 0 | 0 |
| Frozen Coke | Lg | 113 | 455 | 0 | 0 | 0 | 0 |
| Frozen Minute Maid Cherry | Sm | 92 | 370 | 0 | 0 | 0 | 0 |
| Frozen Minute Maid Cherry | Lg | 113 | 450 | 0 | 0 | 0 | 0 |
| Hi-C | Sm | 44 | 160 | 0 | 0 | 0 | 30 |
| Hi-C | Md | 64 | 240 | 0 | 0 | 0 | 40 |
| Hi-C | Lg | 94 | 350 | 0 | 0 | 0 | 60 |
| Iced Tea | Sm | 0 | 0 | 0 | 0 | 0 | 10 |
| Iced Tea | Md | 0 | 0 | 0 | 0 | 0 | 15 |
| Iced Tea | Lg | 0 | 0 | 0 | 0 | 0 | 20 |
| Milk- 1% Lowfat | 8 oz | 13 | 100 | 0 | 10 | 3 | 115 |
| Orange Juice | Sm | 33 | 140 | 0 | 0 | 0 | 5 |
| Orange Juice | Md | 42 | 180 | 0 | 0 | 0 | 5 |
| Orange Juice | Lg | 57 | 250 | 0 | 0 | 0 | 10 |
| Pepsi | Sm | 37 | 140 | 0 | 0 | 0 | 35 |
| Pepsi | Md | 47 | 180 | 0 | 0 | 0 | 45 |

## DRINKS - *cont.*

| | Size | Carb (g) | Cal. (g) | Fiber (g) | Total Chol. (mg) | Fat (g) | Sod. (mg) |
|---|---|---|---|---|---|---|---|
| Pepsi | Lg | 74 | 280 | 0 | 0 | 0 | 70 |
| Sprite | Sm | 40 | 150 | 0 | 0 | 0 | 55 |
| Sprite | Md | 50 | 210 | 0 | 0 | 0 | 80 |
| Sprite | Lg | 75 | 310 | 0 | 0 | 0 | 115 |

# A Word From the Author

Do you lead a busy, active life? I do, too. At least I used to. That active life abruptly changed after I was hit by a truck in a traffic accident. I faced a lengthy battle to recover my mobility and heal from injuries. Overnight, my family became dependent on restaurant foods, especially convenient fast foods. My spatula-wielding days were over, at least for a while. As I was recovering, I became determined to keep us well-fed, healthy and trim. I worked on a plan.

I've always been interested in cooking and nutrition, which ultimately lead to a career in the health and wellness field. For five years I was executive producer and host of the Dallas-Ft. Worth talk radio show *Healthline*, which focused on lifestyle and nutrition. I collected a wealth of information from experts in the medical field during the shows' interviews, and I listened as callers talked about their struggles with weight, what worked and what did not.

I have always been a believer in restricting carbohydrates, intrigued with the high protein, low carbohydrate theory that began decades ago with nutritional pioneers like Adelle Davis. As a working parent who loved to cook, we ate very nutritious, diet-friendly meals - typically high protein, low carbohydrate. But we also relied on fast food and often! I liked the convenience, the taste and the cost. Yet, as a health and nutrition consultant and a mom, I wanted to know exactly what was *in* our food. I did not intend to be blindsided by faux-healthy junk food.

That's how my Fast Food Nutrition Guides were born. Perhaps you have seen them in pharmacies or health food stores. My goal was and still is: *spell out the fast food facts*. Now, after the accident, I had no choice but to refine my own fast food strategies. I wanted to share with others like *you* that it is possible to eat at fast food restaurants and get healthy, non-fattening meals. I also wanted to give you the key to knowing what you are getting in those foods.

Feedback was dramatic as people told me of their shock at discovering the calories, carbohydrate and fat levels in the foods they had been eating. They also related their new feelings of empowerment. They were getting leaner and healthier. So were their children.

Others have added valuable suggestions along the way, and the demand for this information has grown beyond my wildest dreams. I'm trusting that you too will find exactly what you need in *The Low Carb Fast Food Diet* to help you lose weight while enjoying the fun, flavor and convenience of fast foods. Best of all, now you'll have the assurance that you are making healthier choices for yourself and your loved ones.

*~ Carla*